A TRAILS BOOKS GUIDE

TWIN CITIES

RESTAURANT GUIDE

CARLA WALDEMAR

TRAILS BOOKS
Black Earth, Wisconsin

Library of Congress Control Number: 2005904470
ISBN: 1-931599-61-0

Editor: Mark Knickelbine
Design: Jennifer Jackson
Cover Photo: Courtesy Morton's, the Steakhouse

Printed in the United States of America by McNaughton & Gunn, Inc.
10 09 08 07 06 05   6 5 4 3 2 1

TRAILS BOOKS
A division of Trails Media Group, Inc.
P.O. Box 317 • Black Earth, WI 53515
(800) 236-8088 • e-mail: books@wistrails.com
www.trailsbooks.com

TWIN CITIES
RESTAURANT GUIDE

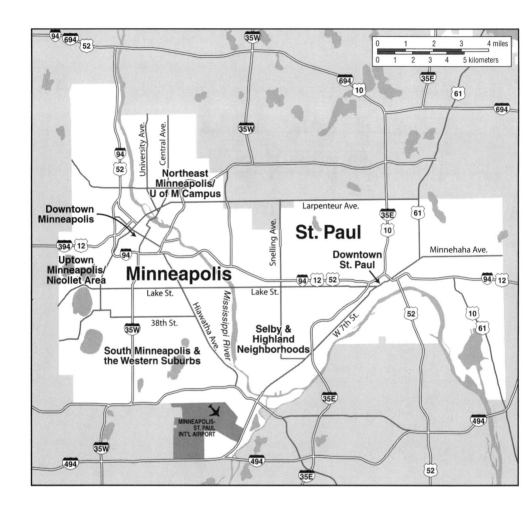

CONTENTS

INTRODUCTION

IT'S BEEN MY good fortune to review Twin Cities restaurants for 25 years. To answer the two most frequent readers' questions: No, I never get tired of dining out, and yes, I really do clean my plate.

To answer the inevitable third query—What's your favorite?—I counter with, "What's your favorite movie/book/child?" It's impossible to select a single haunt. Each has its forte. One may provoke a sense of mystery and adventure, another the comfort of familiar fare well done. One propels me to don fancy duds in anticipation of a night of glitter and polish; another represents a casual neighborhood kitchen where I can count on enjoying an impromptu feast. One fulfils its promise of the best prime rib in town; another, the primo goat curry. I celebrate each café for what it does best—value for money spent, whether a lot or a little—with an eye to an inviting setting, interesting wines, and service that's both informed and accommodating.

During those 25 years of raising a fork for a living, I've seen legends made, or fade; styles change (goodbye, tableside Caesar salad and flaming desserts; hello, open kitchens and soy-glazed tuna); and an exciting new parade of ethnic and regional flavors coming our way. To share my enthusiasm for the quality and diversity of the homegrown dining scene, I've compiled this guide to well over one hundred restaurants that represent the best of the best. Happy dining!

A Note about Symbols:

Prices are indicated by dollar signs ($):
$ (entrées $7 and under)
$$ (entrées $15 and under)
$$$ (entrées $25 and under)
$$$$ (entrées over $25)

P   indicates free parking
O   indicates outdoor seating
M   indicates live entertainment
F   indicates particularly suited to families

All restaurants accept credit cards unless specifically noted. All serve alcohol unless noted. While none require reservations unless noted, it's strongly advised to call ahead.

CHAPTER ONE

Downtown Minneapolis

510 RESTAURANT

510 Groveland Avenue, Minneapolis
(612) 874-6440 • 510restaurant.com
$$; valet parking

IT BLAZED A PATH when it opened back in 1978. The 510, launched by dining devotee Gordon Schutte, was the first restaurant of its kind in the city to meticulously prepare cuisine in the French manner, burying once and for all the misguided notion that "continental" cuisine was the epitome of a dining experience.

The 510's dignified setting, on the ground floor of a patrician residence hotel at the confluence of the Walker Art Center and Loring Park, once set the tone for an evening out, complete with formally trained, tux-clad servers.

But times and tastes have changed, and, though the metamorphosis is still something of a well-kept secret, the 510 has changed as well. Today its ownership has passed to Gordon's son, Brad Schutte, who also serves as chef. To make the experience more open and inviting to all, he's freshened the décor a bit, while wisely retaining the room's intimate, rococo charm. These days the walls have been brightened to a pearly white, and the tables are set with style but less formality; the tuxes have long disappeared. Dainty moldings, gracefully dressed windows, beaded chandeliers, mirrored walls lining the entry, and tasteful touches of growing greenery remain, still setting the mood for a special dining experience.

What's constant is the fine cooking, although it's segued to a somewhat simpler style as well. Escargot en croute remains among the starters, joined now by lobster risotto cakes with sweet red pepper coulis; croustades spread with chicken liver, dried apricots, caramelized onions, and arugula; an enticing salad of grapefruit and craisins joining a warm round of pistachio-coated goat cheese atop field greens, or the evening's soup selection.

Seven entrées vie for diners' votes, and the pan-seared duck breast, served with a warm cranberry-fig compote, wins many of them. So does the rack of lamb in dijon-hazelnut crust and the citrus-glazed salmon, coated simply with a lemon-herb beurre blanc.

To engage both first-timers here to experiment as well as seasoned regulars who dine here on business or pleasure pursuits several times a month, the 510 offers a special three-course menu at an extraordinary value, composed of the soup du jour, a salad of field greens in champagne vinaigrette, and a choice of citrus-kissed salmon, linguine (often prepared with wild mushrooms, arugula, goat cheese and white truffle oil, as answer to a vegetarian's prayers), or a chicken dish that Brad has complemented with Madeira, wild mushrooms, and a leek cream sauce.

The 510's wine list has seen a renaissance, too. These days there are plenty of interesting bottles offered at under $30, along with pours by the glass. Or choose a Rolling Rock, for heaven's sake—something never stocked in the "olden days."

BABALU

800 Washington Avenue North, Minneapolis
(612) 746-5235 • babalu@us
$$$; M

ALL DRESSED UP and at last, somewhere to go. Babalu is the nightclub that the city's sophisticates didn't know they needed until it opened with a flourish in 2003, importing steamy touches of Miami and Old Havana to Minneapolis's Warehouse District. From that day forward, it's been the place to kick back as they do in the tropics, and savor whatever the night might bring.

A large part of the club's allure is in the torrid décor, the vision of three Latino partners who transformed a warehouse off the beaten path into a destination that people beat a path to. Potted palms sway on the sidewalk. Inside, massive wooden ceiling beams and burly pillars, relics of the warehouse days, lend the room a hint of history. Lazing ceiling fans and louvered shutters convey an almost-decadent air of southern climes, accented by walls in stunning tones of burnt orange, eggplant, and ochre. They're hung with pop art portraits of entertainers such as Carmen Miranda and Desi Arnaz, who might feel right at home here, performing on the tiny stage in the rear, where Latin rhythms coax couples to their feet to dance. The bar in the center of the dark, shadowy environs is flanked by opulent lounges, making it tempting to enjoy a Cuba Libre or Mohito "el original."

Or move to a table (which can be noisy, once the music starts) and summon some tapas for starters. The list meanders from mussels to a toss of tiger shrimp, chorizo, and aged sherry; to croquetas of ham or chicken with a lusty, garlic-laced brava sauce; or bites of Spanish manchego cheese. The larger appetizer list continues the meal with offerings like empanadillas stuffed with beef or chicken, calamari bathed in garlic, scallops glazed with Old Havana rum, a tasting of lobster medallions mingling with sweet corn in a smoked paprika butter, and picadillo-stuffed potatoes.

Black bean soup or a bisque of corn and coconut milk ease the path to entrées, as do salads such as roasted beets with avocados or a trio of mangos, tomatoes, and red onions. House specialties reflect the Caribbean, leading off with Cuban-style roast pork and red snapper Veracruz style. Sea bass sports a sauce of pumpkin seeds, jicama, and mango. Grouper merits a coating of plantains along with a guava-habanero sauce from Santiago de Cuba. Cazuela, the traditional seafood casserole, and paella (which must be ordered a day in advance) recreate travelers' favorites seldom found in this city. Sides, if you're still hungry, range from fried yucca to rice and black beans.

Fair warning: The tres leches, a sponge cake laced with three kinds of milk, is downright addictive. But then, so is the orange and coconut flan. Those with more restraint soothe their palates with sorbets in tropical flavors like mango, lemon-melon, and guava-strawberry.

Wines from Argentina, Chile, and Spain are natural choices, but other leading wine regions get their share of attention, too, as do Jamaican, Mexican, and Cuban beers and those sensuous cocktails the Latins do so well.

BELLANOTTE

600 Hennepin Avenue, Minneapolis
(612) 339-7200 • www.Bellanottempls.com
$$$; valet parking; M

BELLANOTTE—"beautiful evening"—is the promise of the new Italian restaurant that spiffed up the dining options in downtown's newly energized Block E in 2004. In fact, it's the block's best real estate for people-watching, with its hundred-seat patio, complete with limestone fountain, that surveys the Target Center and is also near the equally suave and stylish Le Meridien Hotel. The owners, though novices in the restaurant business, have done the extensive R & D required to justify their $3.5 million investment and ensure their place is no mere passing fancy for the multitudes of Beautiful People who've proved eager to drive back in from the burbs to secure a dinner table.

There's a seat for everyone, it seems—snazzy stools at the underlit bar hewn from slabs of honey onyx, tables clustered around a pair of smoldering fire pits and a Vegas-style wine tower, seats close to the working kitchen, and the walk-up pizza station that's fueled by a woodburning oven. All are dressed in changing mood lighting that accents the high-style, Milano-meets-Miami setting created by a noted South Beach consultant. The ambient music also changes as the night wears on, picking up in energy for the late-night crowd.

Bellanotte's menu spans the boot from Napoli's southern cooking to Venezia's refined, high-style dishes. Starters gambol from rustic classics like eggplant parmigiana, mozzarella in carrozza (crisp-fried breaded cheese, served here with a wild mushroom ragout and Bellanotte's signature red sauce) to an elegant tuna tartare spritzed with champagne vinaigrette. From hearty bread salad and a pasta e fagiole soup (like grandma's) to a frisky Caesar or spinach salad as modern updates, the menu progresses to a sextet of stone-fired pizzas and a roll call of pasta dishes. The kitchen's most popular request is the lobster-filled ravioli, closely followed by spinach ravioli plumped with butternut squash in sage brown butter laced with pumpkinseed oil. Or choose a burly plate of lasagna or a spicier toss of linguine with littleneck clams abetted by garlic and crushed red pepper.

Entrées cover the culinary terrain as well, from a rich and hearty chicken Marsala and a giant's portion of osso buco to seafood with a decided flair, such as sole franchese, simply glossed with lemon-caper butter. Of course, there's a beefsteak, Tuscan-style, mighty popular with the Minnesota Timberwolves players who nip over from Target Center after a home NBA game.

And then, desserts! Bellanotte's kitchen fashions a pair of crisp cannoli shells, plump with a filling of ricotta stirred with mascarpone. But don't disregard the tiramisu: It's one of the best in town.

That 1,000-bottle wine tower earns its keep, offering wines poured by the glass from a lengthy list of Italian and California vintners.

BUCA DI BEPPO

1204 Harmon Place, Minneapolis
(612) 288-0138 • bucadibeppo.com
$$; P; F

Additional locations:
14300 Burnhaven Drive, Burnsville • (952) 892-7272
7711 Mitchell Road, Eden Prairie • (952) 934-9463
2728 Gannon Road, Saint Paul • (651) 772-4388
12650 Elm Creek Boulevard North, Maple Grove • (763) 494-3466

BUCA DI BEPPO translates as "Joe's Basement," and, true to its name, it's the Twin Cities' answer to a Chicago speakeasy. The tongue you've got to speak here is Italian—or, make that "Eye-talian," in this send up of all the stereotypical icons of Napoli. High class it ain't: Think high kitsch. That's the charm that has ricocheted this hometown venture, launched in 1993 in downtown Minneapolis, into first a local chain, then a national network all across the country. Mamma mia would be proud.

Expect plastic grapevines, checkered tablecloths, straw-covered bottles of cheap Chianti, and someone crooning "That's Amore" on the sound system— and those are just the tasteful touches. You'll also find a portrait of the Pope painted on a dinner plate and framed "testimonials" from "regulars" like Thelma, the "office temp," and Angie, an "official Tupperware hostess." Michelangelo's naked Adam is portrayed, Sistine-style, handing his Creator a green can of Parmesan; Eve is painted leaving Eden with a Buca doggie bag.

Parties of families or office friends flock here to have a grand old time, and it just so happens that grand food and grand service are a big part of the bargain. Warrens of small rooms hung with twinkling Christmas lights, each room with its own blackboard menu, set the stage for summoning ample portions of hearty southern Italian staples, served family-style, con gusto. Pizza as big as a bathmat makes the perfect starter, relayed from the kitchen to take center stage on a plank propped up by a couple of tomato cans. Vino served from gallon jugs. You get the idea.

Choose an overflowing salad to pass around the table, then a couple of hearty pastas and perhaps chicken cacciatore—that's the whole bird smothered in red sauce. Red sauce rules here.

So does attitude. If the waiters aren't in the employ of the Mafia, they're adept pretenders. And they make the evening.

CAFÉ BRENDA

300 First Avenue North, Minneapolis
(612) 342-9230 • www.cafebrenda.com
$$; P

BRENDA LANGTON, who turned 46 in 2004, has been riding the range in her own café kitchen for 25 years—and if you do the math, you'll realize she opened her first restaurant at age 21. Working in a food co-op since age 15 led her to champion natural and vegetarian foods while learning how a business runs. Bravely, she cracked a nest egg of $5,000 to open Café Kardemena in Saint Paul. It proved to be a hit, especially with folks across the river, so moving to Minneapolis to grow the business was a no-brainer. She found a street-corner space in the Warehouse District "that reminded me of Greens, the San Francisco vegetarian restaurant, so I decided, 'That's it!'"

Like its role model on the bay, the high ceiling, minimalist white walls, and expanse of windows at Café Brenda create a light and airy ambience, the better to showcase Brenda's unique fare and the movers and shakers of the arts and corporate world who flock here to eat it up. And, just as this space is more, well, genteel than the funky digs that got Brenda started, her menu, too, has migrated from the sprouts-and-tofu circuit on which she put her stamp. The service, while as friendly as always, has become as polished as in any downtown contender.

These days, inspired by cuisines worldwide, but particularly the sunny Mediterranean, Brenda offers chicken and fish, including trout from Wisconsin's Star Prairie showcased in entrées like trout stuffed with smoked trout mousse, or sesame-crusted arctic char swimming in a bowl of savory Chinese noodles and vegetables in an aromatic ginger broth. And her addictive cornbread is the first thing to hit the table to fortify diners as they make hard choices.

Rice and lentils, sure, but there's also Southwestern mock-duck tacos and Japanese chilled-noodle salad slithering with a peanut satay sauce, served on greens dressed with preserved lemon. There's even a Brenda Burger, fashioned of vegetables, brown rice, and nuts but garnished with the familiar lettuce, pickle, and catsup. Meal-size salads are more than a pretty picture, too. And her wild mushroom-pistachio pate, served with cranberry chutney and mustard sauce, could rival that of any gourmet kitchen.

Brenda's mission remains: Encourage people to eat healthily by providing stunning teasers to their eyes and palates, but without the use of sugar, white flour, and other refined and processed products.

Behind the token service bar, hand-set with tiny tiles, Brenda's husband, Tim, manages the front of the house, greeting regulars, taking coats, and suggesting specials. Together the couple has assembled an unusual and intriguing wine list at good value, including offerings by Minnesota's own Alexis Bailly Winery (see sidebar), backed by a handpicked list of micro beers. Brenda also has started preparing healthy meals for in-home clients, particularly boomers who fret about the specter of a heart attack. And she's also working on an update of her seminal *Café Brenda Cookbook*, rumor has it.

CAFÉ LURCAT

1624 Harmon Place, Minneapolis
(612) 486-5500 • damico.com
$$; valet parking; O; M

WHERE DID ALL the Beautiful People go? One peek inside Café Lurcat and the mystery's cleared up: right here. The setting's pretty gorgeous, too, in a site anchoring the top end of pretty little Loring Park. A patio captures the view all summer, and the rest of the year the views can be seen from round

HELL'S KITCHEN

89 South 10th Street • Minneapolis • (612) 332-4700

"Serving damn good food" is the motto of longtime friends, chefs, and co-owners Mitch Omer and Steve Meyer, who opened this tiny downtown Minneapolis breakfast and lunch spot in May 2002. Giving the slogan "power breakfast" a whole new meaning, they serve the city's movers and shakers such potent day-starters as a bison strip steak Benedict with tangerine-jalapeno hollandaise, a steamy bowl of Manhomin porridge composed of wild rice, blueberries, cranberries, and toasted hazelnuts topped with cream and maple syrup, and lemon-ricotta pancakes for those with puny appetites. The pair has worked together at Pracna on Main, the Pickled Parrot, and the New French Café, all shuttered these days, but clearly primo training ground for homemade everything: peanut butter, ketchup, marmalade, you name it. The décor, wouldn't you know, includes a collection of Gary Larson's cartoons from hell.

the bar, with its informal seating and menu, to the vast, uncluttered windows of the restaurant itself.

The décor is as contemporary as the food savants who eat here: a chocolate-toned ceiling sailing high above blond wood floors, bounded by the white-white-white that spans the walls and filmy curtains and flows onto a sea of starched tablecloths and slipcovered chairs. Here and there, uncovered brick archways add a patina to the contemporary aura, and in the rear an open kitchen stretches unobtrusively.

Servers, whose chocolate shirts match the ceiling, are well equipped to offer friendly advice about the menu—a refreshingly straightforward list that harks back to simpler days before trendy showmanship caught on. It's all orchestrated by Jay Sparks, one of the D'Amico restaurant group's shining stars. But the simplicity is deceiving; expect a little unannounced coup de grâce on every plate.

Entrées—not more than a dozen or so—are listed under various headings, like "Saute" (ahi tuna with lemon confit); "Roasts" (farmhouse chicken in honey and cider vinegar sauce), "Braises" (pot roast simmered in red wine), and "Broiler & Grill," where you'll find both a simple hanger steak and filet of Kobe beef. Vegetables and starches are listed à la carte to allow you to pick and choose favorites from the likes of asparagus roasted with garlic butter, pan-fried gnocchi, stoneground grits, and roasted cauliflower.

Starters are equally to the point: raw and cold dishes include tartares of salmon, tuna, or beefsteak, as well as oysters on the half-shell and Lurcat's spin on a classic shrimp cocktail. Among the hot appetizers, crab cakes rule, sided with a sassy aioli. Salads present more classics fine-tuned for today: whole leaves of romaine with a Green Goddess dressing (gulp! How long since we've seen that on a sophisticated menu?) and a Parisian bistro toss of bacon and poached egg on baby greens among them.

Cheese makes a superb dessert here, and guests are treated to a sampler plate of five artisanal varieties snagged from all over the world. If it's a sweet you crave, the restaurant again takes a back-to-the-basics approach with treats like a chocolate–peanut butter torte, rhubarb tart, or the offering that most sorely tests dieters' resistance, a plate of warm, cinnamon-sugar mini-doughnuts just like you'd find at the State Fair (but, need we add, better).

Add in an intelligent, eclectic wine list of 200 bottles, with over 30 offered by the glass at a fair value, and it's clear why those snazzy, House Beautiful–type chairs are regularly in demand.

COSMOS

Hotel Le Meridien, 601 First Avenue North, Minneapolis
(612) 312-1168 • cosmosrestaurant.com
$$$; valet parking

WHAT GIVENCHY IS TO WOMEN'S FASHION, Cosmos is to restaurant design—cool, expensive, sophisticated. It's the fine-dining venue of Le Meridien, the cities' new and unquestionably most haute hotel, incongruously located in the anything-but-haute Block E. (Whisk up to the fourth floor, however, and you'll immediately forget you're next door to Planet Hollywood.)

Here the backlit bar, not out of place in London or New York, sizzles with supermodels and their squires, and beyond it, the lofty dining room beckons—a minimalist study in a near-monochromatic palette of natural wood, silvery drapes above dove-gray banquettes, and a black wall studded with what looks like a hundred mirrored portholes. Servers, cloaked in black, pad softly through the shadows. Tables, in the same rare Indonesian wood as those expansive walls, are mirrored by tawny marble floors. Tables are sparely set as well: no flowers, no candles, no cloths—simply clear glass service plates and wine stems.

What steals the limelight is the food. Chef Seth Bixby Daugherty, an alum of D'Amico Cucina, lends his discernment to this kitchen in dishes that dazzle the eyes as well as the taste buds. Portions are sane, not Minnesota-mammoth, so it's possible to amble through several courses with comfort.

Appetizers include sweetbreads set upon a velvety puree of cauliflower; a generous slice of Hudson Valley foie gras paired with fruit of the season—pineapple, rhubarb, or figs; and a "soup" of several giant diver scallops swimming in miso broth flavored with cucumber, onion, and Asian herbs.

Salads, to share or pair, range from simple gathered greens to elaborate assemblies such as duck confit with frisee, watercress, preserved tomatoes, and the dainty poached egg of a quail. The most popular salad plate, Seth confesses, is his combination of poached lobster with Fuji apple, aged ricotta cheese, and a truffled dwarf peach that sets heads turning with its fragrance.

Seth focuses his attention on ten entrées. It's hard to beat the crisp-skinned black sea bass sent out with a morel-tomato tart and braised asparagus—proof that less is indeed more—or chicken atop a morel and spring pea risotto. Star Prairie trout, flash-fried tempura-style, rates sushi rice, soy sauce, and lemony olive oil as its accessories, while a wild boar chop fares well beside a sweet-potato cake and a splash of veal jus.

Desserts take on more caprice, or strangeness, depending on one's tolerance for coupling. Consider a brown-sugar spice cake wrapped in phyllo pastry brushed with orange marmalade, or a cinnamon cheesecake that claims a jalapeno and cream cheese fritter, chipotle caramel, and ice cream as its mates. Well, there's always chocolate—here in the form of a dense, delicious, flourless bite of cake topped with dual mousses of raspberry and mango.

Plenty of wines by the glass are listed, along with a handful of half-bottles for those who love to mix and match. The suits who lunch here are treated to many of the same dishes, as well as sandwiches and an expanded list of salads.

DAKOTA JAZZ CLUB AND RESTAURANT

1010 Nicollet Mall, Minneapolis
(612) 332-1010 • dakotacooks.com
$$–$$$; O; M; valet parking

WELL, IT'S ABOUT TIME, said the many loyal fans of the Dakota, when the bar/restaurant/music venue moved in 2004 from its original location in Saint Paul's Bandana Square—once lively, now a tomb—to downtown Minneapolis. The

Dakota adopted a prime location on Nicollet Mall, reversing the fate of two failed predecessors and giving the site a sleek look all its own, as sophisticated as the national jazz names who play here and as pared-down and natural as the kitchen's signature cooking.

Diners may choose a roomy booth, a table at the tightly packed bar close to the stage (unless they wish to carry on a conversation), or mezzanine seating, from which to survey the stage (and, as Shakespeare observed, we're all players in this scene). There's a cleverly designed folding wall separating the dining area from the music arena that disappears after the dinner hour to allow a view of the stage from all seats.

Some menu items have been revised, some added, and some hallowed dishes kept intact. Yet the cafe retains its strong, 20-year commitment to seek out and showcase regional producers. They mean it: no lobster, no spaghetti, no papaya. Instead, you'll find Boundary Waters walleye, wild rice, and Minnesota apples. Dishes are kept simple in order to let the stars—the ingredients themselves—shine through.

The Dakota's legendary brie-apple soup, based on cheese from Wisconsin, still holds a place of honor, and it's as rich and velvety as ever. The Caesar salad—a benchmark for all others around town—still has a garlicky kick. A starter plate of smoked salmon and sturgeon, served with apple-celery slaw and sour cherries, is as spot-on as it sounds.

So is anything the chef creates with walleye. Diners may test this claim with a bowl of walleye and smoked whitefish chowder, laced with wild rice. Or choose for a starter the broiled walleye in pumpkin seeds with mashed root vegetables, a currant-pear glaze, and leeks. Warning: The smoked Star Prairie trout and goat cheese flan is just as tasty, fueled with horseradish, apples, and red onions. Or go for either fish as an entrée—trout with dried tomato butter, or the walleye with a snappy mustard-horseradish sauce. Carnivores will appreciate a prime rib of local Pipestone pork roasted with dried berries or a beef strip loin basted in Hastings Reserve wine from Alexis Bailly Winery.

New to this incarnation of the Dakota's menu is a short, sweet list entitled "American comfort food," such as mac and cheese gone uptown with black trumpet mushrooms, chicken pot pie gussied up with chanterelles, and a bison/bacon meatloaf served with barbecue gravy and—what else?—mashed potatoes.

The dessert list just doesn't quit. Amid the dozen-plus items made in-house, choose the signature maple frango served with blueberry syrup, sour cream, and buckwheat wafers or the pear and dried-blueberry crisp under vanilla ice cream. The banana caramel cake is State Fair quality, and the root beer float, made with 1919 root beer from a Minnesota maker, has its devotees.

The Dakota's wine list is intelligent and just as purpose-driven as the food.

D'AMICO CUCINA

Butler Square, 100 North Sixth Street, Minneapolis
(612) 338-2401 • damico.com
$$$$; valet parking; M

THE D'AMICO BROTHERS (Richard, the design guru, and Larry, chef extraordinaire) led the way in guiding Midwestern palates to fine dining, Italian-style. Before them, red sauce and checked tablecloths; after, true gourmet fare in a setting that could turn heads in Milano, Italy's most fashion-forward city. With foresight, the brothers took over a location in the Warehouse District's Butler Square, whose exposed-brick walls and heavy wooden ceiling beams have been declared historically preserved. Juxtaposing old and new, the cleanly designed, cosmopolitan interior showcases well-spaced tables, simply clad in white, stylish chrome-and-leather chairs, and walls and carpet in soft, neutral tones (mushroom? putty?). White sheers frame the oversize windows, Oriental rugs add accents to the carpets, and brass chandeliers swing from the "industrial" ceiling, just like in a Fellini movie.

In the back lies an appealing private dining room, and at the entrance there's a sleek bar, complete with cushy armchairs and a grand piano. No bones about it: D'Amico Cucina is decidedly a special-occasion restaurant—a destination for sealing business deals or celebrating milestones. But it's far too appealing to be saved for twice a year. One doesn't need an excuse to treat oneself to the imaginative and meticulously prepared wonders that emerge from the kitchen—simply a well-lined pocket. The experience is enhanced by one of the most polished, engaging, and discreet waitstaffs in town.

They're more than eager to describe every last detail of the menu's fixings, beginning with antipasti such as foie gras with Mission figs, onions, and walnut biscotti or tuna tartare paired with cucumber and grapefruit pearls. Among the primi, or pasta numbers, that jump off the list are ravioli filled with house-made ricotta in a black truffle butter; fresh tagliolini with Manila clams, pancetta, white wine, and tomatoes; or a Milanese risotto with braised oxtail, sun-dried tomatoes, and green olives.

Secondi, the main plates, run the gamut from butter-poached chicken with morels and a chive risotto to braised lamb with cannelini beans and swiss chard or grilled bone-in pork chops sided with sautéed peaches and polenta enriched with the pungent flavor of Gorgonzola cheese.

Desserts are considered part of the food pyramid by the Cucina's astute diners, especially when the list includes crème fraiche custards under a sherry glaze

13

and crust of glazed pecans, or a warm peach-hazelnut crostata scented with lime butter and served with mascarpone sorbet and Italian meringue. Or be surprised and summon the assortment of individual chocolate pastries to share over a sip or two of espresso.

A five-course tasting menu puts the decision into the hands of the talented chef; wine pairings are optional. It's a grand way to get a feel for what the kitchen is in love with at the moment, and makes for a most romantic evening. Of course, the wine list is a hymn to all that's fine to drink in Italy, and priced accordingly.

FIRELAKE

Radisson Plaza Hotel, 31 South Seventh Street, Minneapolis
(612) 216-3974 • www.firelakerestaurant.com
$$; valet parking

THE DOWNTOWN MINNEAPOLIS Radisson Plaza Hotel—flagship of the worldwide Radisson empire—made a bold move in mid-2004. It put to rest its fine-dining room and opened a casual, more contemporary street-side café. It's a lesson in our changing times, and it's working. Firelake, dressed in warm cinnamon tones, is more suited for business folk or ballgame fans than divas. The best seats are the curvy, faux-leather booths that serve as box seats for the stage performance in the form-follows-function open kitchen in the rear.

Executive chef Paul Lynch, once head of the former Festival Room upstairs, has simplified the menu without dumbing it down, thus retaining his edge in culinary marriage-making.

Take the starters, for example. The walleye/scallion/wild rice fritters nearly float on air, they're so light. And the alder-smoked salmon trout is nearly as addictive, paired with slices of grilled bruschetta and a plate painting of orange and black pepper aioli so good it ought to be patented. Beer-battered shrimp earn an upgrade with sherry-scallion sauce, and mesquite-grilled chicken sticks become more than bar food when steeped in a yogurt marinade and sent out with a spicy buttermilk harissa dipping sauce.

Meal-sized salads show Lynch's way of defying expectations. His "gathered greens" share company with Minnesota Amablu cheese, apples, and walnuts in a spritz of sherry vinegar, while his Minnesota bread salad is pure genius in a bowl: greens sequined with cranberries, wild rice croutons, Stickney Hill cheese, bacon, tomato, corn, and more, all baptized with balsamic vinegar. Or if it's soup you're craving, settle on the Minnesota mushroom, leek, and wild rice version that's the kitchen's specialty.

Sandwiches include a walleye burger, an old-fashioned club, and a portobello and prime rib duo, while the entrée list encourages diners to choose between pasta preparations and an A list of steaks, chops, and seafood. The honey-cured, pecan-smoked pork chop, a double cut served bone-in, shares its plate with maple-glazed yams and apples, while the cornflour-crusted Iroquois walleye is honored with a homemade remoulade, the fancy French version of plain ol' tartar sauce. The rotisserie on view behind the counter works wonders on a Minnesota-grown chicken rubbed with rosemary and garlic. It's served with a cheddar-herb mash that makes you want to lick your plate.

Lots of fancy coffee drinks head the dessert list, but beyond the Starbucks treats you'll discover more substantial sweets such as a suave crème caramel and poached pear combo, a chai-spiced Bundt cake sided with pumpkin semifreddo, and a cheesecake fashioned of lightweight ricotta laced with pine nuts. If this is modern hotel dining, it's about time!

GOODFELLOW'S

City Center, 40 South Seventh Street, Minneapolis
(612) 332-4800 • goodfellowsrestaurant.com
$$$$; valet parking

TOPPING MANY A LIST of fine-dining favorites, Goodfellow's has long set the standard for fresh, seasonal cuisine with a regional emphasis. Enveloped in a delightful mantle of déjà vu, the restaurant occupies the site of the long-gone but fondly remembered Forum Cafeteria, an icon of the 30s. Repositioned after years in storage, its Art Deco embellishments have been restored in their original setting.

Pale aqua walls showcase the arresting period ZigZag mirrors below a ceiling similarly bathed in pale blue, crisscrossed with geometric silver streaks and punctuated by museum-quality etched-glass chandeliers. Wheat motifs abound as salutes to Minnesota's position as breadbasket for the nation, from sheaves decorating the series of angular octagonal pillars to ebony-toned, eye-level tiles in the dining room. From the balcony in the rear, where private parties gather, to the overstuffed furniture in the foyer, the air is one of sophistication and comfort.

Tables are generously spaced to allow business guests their privacy, and waiters are cued to serve discreetly, interrupting only when their sense of timing dictates that diners are ready for their attention. Trust these servers on the wine list, unless you have endless hours to peruse the monumental book.

They're adroit guides to the specialties of the kitchen, too, although the simple menu almost guarantees that every dish is given its due attention. A surprise *amuse*—a tidbit sent out as gift of the chef—rehearses one's palate for the good things to follow. His list of small plates entice with simple but inspired pairings, like smoked local trout with Asian pears and horseradish or the popular Boston lettuce salad with buttermilk blue cheese, pears, and walnuts.

Lovers of foie gras will find the supple goose liver paired with acidic fruit, such as maple-glazed apples, to complement its richness. Fancy. But then, there's a spice-rubbed spring hen paired with a rustic bread salad and currants— simple and satisfying.

Nueske's bacon, the best in these parts, is drafted to wrap pork tenderloin plated with wild rice and mustard greens, another entrée that never gets uppity, although the taste is close to heaven. Or vote for the rabbit, served with wild mushrooms, spring peas, and dark ale—again uncontrived yet unbeatable. And if it's fish you fancy, consider grilled halibut with asparagus and sweet Manila clams.

Goodfellows' new pastry chef, who hails from Chicago's acclaimed Tru, as does the chef, continues the tradition of excellence. Fruit pastries are her forte, according to most reviews. Should your taste buds crave a savory finale, Goodfellow's is one of the few local restaurants to offer a selection of artisanal cheeses.

IKE'S FOOD AND COCKTAILS

50 South 6th Street, Minneapolis
(612) 746-4537 • ilikeikes.com
$-$$

IKE'S, POSITIONED NEXT TO MURRAY'S, the venerable steakhouse, looks like it's been part of the downtown neighborhood for just as many decades. But no—it was built from the ground up in 2003 in a narrow corridor where once an alley wandered. Thanks to clever decorating, the restaurant's atmosphere feels just like the 40s. A working bar bisects the length of the narrow room, with stools where single diners love to perch and chat with the able tenders.

Dark booths line both walls, with quotable sayings—think W. C. Fields— framed above, along with wartime-era posters. And front-and-center at the entrance stands the carver's station, manned by a handsome chef in a starched white hat.

Ike's serves a true downtown crowd—a comfy source of daily breakfast, if a stack of flapjacks, fresh-baked pastry, or bananas on your cereal are your idea of starting the day right before you hit the office. The kitchen does a brisk lunchtime business in burgers and carvery sandwiches, too; it also lures a lively happy-hour crowd, which often lingers on to fill the booths for dinner.

The Angus burger, hand-pattied and served with all the trimmings, reappears in the evening, as do the old-fashioned, extra thick, brain-freezing milkshakes in three flavors. Ike's triple threat chili is served from noon to evening, along with the meal-in-itself chopped salad, which seems to include everything tasty in the entire kitchen, along with warm bread.

Ike's menu was designed by consulting chef Tobie Niditz, veteran of many local dining destinations. Some savvy diners build a meal from the generous listing of small plates, such as balsamic-glazed asparagus, crab cakes with homemade tartar sauce on spicy slaw, and guacamole made to order right before your eyes, served with warm tortilla chips still in the fry basket (that's how fresh they are). The list of small dishes also makes a hit with the late-night crowd who crave fare that takes on a more exotic edge, such as skewers of chicken satay laced with Thai chili oil, pork and vegetable potstickers with dual dips of soy-ginger and sriracha chili sauce, or the pair of mini-sandwiches—one on sourdough, one on pumpernickel—reproduced from the menu of the city's once-famous Charlie's Café, put to rest years ago, but not before Ike's salvaged the the recipe for the seared beef tenderloin in horseradish sauce.

Dinner entrées are limited (who needs them, after all of the above?) to the fish of the day, a bone-in Kansas City Angus strip steak with Ike's addictive fries and onion strings, and the daily blue plate special (if it's meatloaf, dig in).

Desserts? Just two—a New York–style cheesecake topped with berries and what the chef brags is a "ridiculously intense double chocolate" cake in three immense layers, served with your choice of a scoop of Sebastian Joes's primo vanilla ice cream or a tall, frosty glass of milk.

THE LOCAL

931 Nicollet Mall Minneapolis
(612) 904-1000 • www.the-local.com
$–$$; O

THE LOCAL IS MORE than a place to eat and drink; it's Irish, and not your third-generation variety, either. Owner Kieran Folliard hails from the Emerald Isle, and he's recreated a pub/café that, you'd swear by the blarney stone, had flourished for a hundred years in Dublin. Yet here it is, smack on the Nicollet Mall, where it draws more suits than blue collars—and who cares if they're Swedish?

High ceilings above acres of dark wood blend with Irish tunes and lively conversation. They superintend a comfy, street-side corner stocked with sofas, etched glass, hanging plants, and vintage photographs—the makings of a Victorian hotel parlor. But the true altar of worship is the long, double-sided bar behind it—all dusky, carved wood and polished glass, stocked with platoons of whiskey bottles, like Bushmills and Jameson, and close to a dozen beer spigots, of which the Guinness gets the most workout. Cheers, eat your heart out: Minneapolis has The Local.

Just as in Dublin, warrens of alcoves each hold a single table and enough chairs to gather all your friends. Guests can partake in the central action yet carry on, in semi-privacy, the kind of animated conversation that seems a religious calling among the Irish and their local admirers. And in summer—well, as soon as the ice is off the pavement—sidewalk tables increase the ranks of Kieran's devout disciples.

These days Jason Hicks heads up the kitchen, known for its hearty, stick-to-your-ribs Irish food: potato-leek soup, of course, a curried lamb "hand pie" or the vegetarian version of the pastry, plump with spinach and Irish cheddar—oh, and a salad if one must, as starters to precede what Kieran claims to be his "world famous" (would he lie?) fish and chips. Or choose corned beef and cabbage, shepherd's pie of the day, homemade bangers (that's sausage, if you're Swedish) and mash drowned in a tasty onion gravy, meatloaf with a spirited glaze of John Powers Whiskey, or a traditional Irish breakfast—served not only at brunch time, but all day. For dessert, consider the homemade bread pudding or apple tart fueled with another spritz of John Powers, along with caramel sauce.

Luncheon sandwiches are as generous and wholesome as you might expect, and of course, there are those happy-hour teasers to help the Guinness on its way. And here, as you also might expect, happy hour extends far into the late hours of the evening.

Kieran also operates Kieran's Irish Pub at 300 2nd Avenue South, offering live Irish music, poetry slams, and more in another corner of downtown Minneapolis, which celebrated its tenth anniversary in 2004; more recently he opened the Liffey Irish Pub at 175 West 7th Street in downtown Saint Paul, giving his homeboys a place to call their own on that side of the river.

MANNY'S STEAKHOUSE

Hyatt Regency Hotel, 1300 Nicollet Mall, Minneapolis
(612) 339-9900 • mannyssteakhouse.com
$$$$

MANNY'S IS ALL ABOUT BEEF. (Maybe someone ordered chicken once; if so, they're still talking about it in the kitchen.) This is your primal, New York–style steakhouse, where people (make that: business moguls) come to clinch deals over mammoth, test-your-manhood portions of red meat.

The atmosphere is decidedly masculine, too. The tone is set in the arcade, lined with glossy photos of the national superstars, sports heroes, and politicos who have dined within and come away smiling.

Here they skip the violins and flowers and cut to the chase. Like the proverbial Manhattan steakhouses upon which it's patterned, the floor is bare and the walls are landscaped with wine racks holding the sizes and vintages requisite to toast the signing of a contract. The tables, set almost monastically with little except two-fisted steak knives as "theme" décor, are positioned with straight-backed, no-nonsense chairs in close configuration, with just enough space for the butcher cart to circulate.

The cart serves as a show-and-tell menu. Waiters lift each plastic-wrapped cut in turn, extolling the various virtues of strip, filet, rib eye, tenderloin, and porterhouse, along with spuds the size of footballs and asparagus it no doubt took a chain saw to harvest. These pro servers, working the room in their utilitarian gray cotton smocks, are part of the sizzle—nice Minnesota boys trained to impart a little New York lip and attitude (albeit with a wink of an eye). They'll also help you select the best side dishes for the table to share from the straightforward, à la carte menu.

The list leads off with time-tested appetizer classics: oysters on the half-shell, shrimp cocktail, and crab cakes. Then come the mighty meat offerings, some of which do stray beyond beef to include prime lamb, veal and pork chops, lobster, and that token chicken. You'll find none of your baby microgreens on the salads meant for sharing. Instead, the plates include Caesar salad, hearts of palm, and a plate of tomatoes and onions, among the steakhouse standards. Desserts, such as an entire chocolate cake, are just as over the top.

So is the portrait of the bull flaunting his masculinity at the entrance, providing a graphic topic for conversation. The same simple menu is offered in the bar to the left, a smaller, darker, cozier room, which is also done up in classic New York style with red banquettes. Manager Randy Stanley, a longtime figure in the Minneapolis hospitality scene, keeps the whole operation in motion, and makes sure you don't forget your doggie bag. But at these prices, chances are the contents never get to Fido.

MARKET BAR-B-QUE

1414 Nicollet Avenue, Minneapolis
(612) 872-1111

15320 Wayzata Blvd. (Interstate 394), Minnetonka
(952) 475-1770 • marketbbq.com
$$; P; F

THE MARKET IS MORE than a barbecue joint, it's a place of worship. To long-time fans—and they are many—who have followed its move from one location to another over the years, it's been practicing baptism by hickory smoke since 1946. For decades, the logo—a porker in a chef's hat and red neckerchief—has brought culinary salvation to all who seek the real deal. The Market features lean, mahogany racks of ribs slow-smoked over hickory coals till they're redolent with the irresistible aroma of the pit. These are ribs for those who love to wrestle the meat from the bones rather than have it steamed into submission. "Tender" is not an adjective that comes to mind with these ribs; for that, roam elsewhere. "Flavorful" is the word here.

Among those pigging out at hog heaven are swing-shift workers, nationally notable musicians, politicians, and sports heroes passing through town. (You can trace their names embedded on a lineup of special brass plaques; their autographed photos also line the foyer, along with accolades in print from scores of publications.) "Eleven of you? Fine!" agreed the hostess on a recent visit. "I'll set up a round table."

Appearances are deceiving. At first glance, there's a rather bland bar facing Nicollet Avenue, just a couple of blocks before it gussies itself up and morphs into the Nicollet Mall. Head, instead, to the two back rooms with their low, pressed-tin ceilings, checkered oilcloth table covers, and ceiling fans that volley forward the heady perfume from the pit. One room maintains the Market's traditional high-backed, dark, wooden booths, unpadded as a church pew (but an order of ribs will take care of that). The other room maintains a swarm of tables beneath the ranks of neon beer signs on the mirrored walls.

The Market's ribs are served to satisfy the true aficionado—bare, unmasked by sauce. (You can add your choice, from sweet to sassy, on the side.) They're accompanied, ever since the Market began, with nary a nod to trendiness, simply by a mess of fries, a tiny cup of vinegary coleslaw, and slabs of white-bread toast. Yes, you can choose beef ribs if you'd rather, or barbecue in the guise of chicken, sirloin steak, burger, or other combos; there's even a salmon burger, walleye, or fried mozzarella sticks. But why?

MCCORMICK & SCHMICK'S

800 Nicollet Mall, Minneapolis
(612) 338-3300 • mccormickandschmicks.com
$$; O

LOCATION, LOCATION, LOCATION: McCormick & Schmick's has mastered all three essentials of securing prime real estate. Smack in the middle of the meandering Nicollet Mall, it captures traffic—and lots of it—from the office buildings along the street as well as the avenue's platoon of shoppers and playgoers from Hennepin Avenue's theater district a mere two blocks away.

But location isn't enough to keep the fans coming back. They're hooked on the quality and value of the fresh seafood. But that leaves out part of the winning equation, too. This corporation, based in the Pacific Northwest, takes its staff training seriously, turning out the squads of friendly and informed servers you'll spot hoisting platters from the kitchen and oyster station open to view in the rear. Not only are they on first-name terms with the finny fellows listed on the lengthy daily fresh sheet, they're also masters of the art of making sure customers enjoy their meals.

What comes out of a can or package in this demanding kitchen? Well, salt and pepper, not much else. The freezer? Ice cubes, but very little more. Instead, inspect the ranks of close to a dozen varieties of oysters on view in their shells, and note the origin of the fish and shellfish flown in on a daily basis. If the kitchen runs out, it's out—it's that simple. That's why the menu is printed anew twice a day.

Preparations don't disguise the unique taste and texture of each variety, yet the finished product is never boring. Consider Idaho trout, for instance, swathed in ancho-chili butter sauce, or catfish from Arkansas lightly breaded with pecans, with a jalapeno-mango chutney on the side. The steelhead salmon from British Columbia merits a suave horseradish rub, while the fish cakes fashioned from Asian mahimahi are matched with a Thai peanut sauce and lemongrass-jasmine rice. Or try the "true" fish and chips made from Alaskan cod, coated in a local honey-weiss beer batter. Canadian lake trout goes uptown with a compote of apples and dried cherries. And the list goes on, including a home-style meatloaf or a chicken with a ragout of port and wild mushrooms for those who prefer fixings off the farm.

Start with a cup of clam chowder or oyster stew, or perhaps those oysters—on the half-shell or pan-fried with tartar sauce. The crab cakes are good, but the salmon cakes are even better, brightened with green apples and leeks. Sandwiches and entrée salads add to the mix. Desserts—homemade, of course—climax in a tender-crusted apple pie, served with vanilla ice cream. Wines by the glass are routine, while the bottle listing ventures farther.

The series of rooms, done in dark wood punctuated with framed prints, creates a choice of warm, inviting settings, from the private alcove booths along the kitchen to the street-side spaces sprinkled with well-spaced tables, on to the atmospheric, old-style bar that features its own happy hour menu, in service both late afternoon and late evening. And we're not talking chips and dip; rather, you'll find more interesting fare such as fish tacos with black beans, those Asian mahimahi cakes or salmon cakes, and even sloppy joes served, you bet, with fries.

MISSION AMERICAN KITCHEN AND BAR

IDS Center, 80 South Seventh Street, Minneapolis
(612) 339-1000 • www.missionamerican.com
$$–$$$; P

LIKE A CULINARY PHOENIX, Mission was born from the figurative ashes of Aquavit, the high-end, concept-pushing restaurant that never quite felt at home sharing street-level space with the Gap, et al., in the IDS Center. Mission, which opened in summer 2004, has solved the visibility challenge by carving out a street-side entrance and completely rehabbing the interior space. The once-stark interior has been warmed (but not overheated) with earthy tones—mushroom, artichoke, and burnt orange among them—to complement the dark wooden floor and maple-hued tabletops that dot the shadowy open space. Its clean lines are broken simply by a wall-sized sculpted metal hanging and a glassed-in wine room. The bar has been moved closer to the expansive windows, framed in filmy sheers; and it offers its own informal menu of appetizers and desserts.

Chef Jordan Smith, an alum of D'Amico Cucina, guides his crew from a kitchen viewed through a window at the hostess stand. His mission at Mission is to present satisfying, all-American classics in a fresh, light manner. True to our Midwestern expectations, portions are more than ample; it's possible to share plates and still leave sated.

His starters are simple enough: chilled shellfish to summon by the piece; Mission crackers with tomato, basil, and chevre; deviled eggs (really! When's the last time you found those on an upscale menu?); chicken livers with garlic; and a grill of shrimp and spicy sausages on roasted red pepper toast. Salads toe the line, too: a classic chophouse, a Caesar salad, and a toss of feta and warm spinach, or tomato, bacon, and dill are as froufrou as they get.

The entrée list is kept short, abetted by the special of the evening. Always present are a grilled Angus sirloin with eggplant and tomatoes; roast chicken atop a bread salad with arugula; a breaded veal chop spritzed with lemon; country-style pork ribs ready to fall off the bone, served with cilantro rice; and a down-home catfish paired with French fries and tartar sauce. Of the side dishes on offer, the broccoli with garlic is a definite favorite, as are the grilled portobellos, the braised greens spiked with ham, and the buttery mashed baby reds.

Desserts hark back to a golden past as well, starting with a floating island, on to a chocolate soufflé, chocolate cream pie, lemon pudding cake, homey fruit cobbler and, yes, a root beer float. Artisanal cheeses, solo or in a plate of three, also offer a grand way to finish that last sip of red wine. The wine list features a wide-ranging selection of about-to-be-hot global labels and winners from our own shores, offered at fair value. Chef Jordan, who also operates a suburban wine shop, clearly has had a voice in their selection. Now, if only the staff were versed in them as well, along with fine points of the menu. In their dark shirts, pants, and ties, they're an accommodating lot but merit further training on what these lists are all about. Diners here are city slickers, joined by guests from the adjoining Marquette Hotel—a thirties-to-boomer clientele; some have grown kids in tow, discovering a new venue in which to enjoy the better things of life.

MONTE CARLO

219 Third Avenue North, Minneapolis
(612) 333-5900
$-$$; P; F

THE MENU STATES "since 1906," but that's long before seasoned restaurateur John Rimarcik foretold the bar and grill's potential, took the helm, and steered it to SRO status. In the old days, it was a blue-collar bar, well below the foodies' radar. But for decades now, it's been packed from its stamped-tin ceiling to the lino-tiled floor with polished professionals who claim this Warehouse District cubbyhole as their particular haunt. Maybe in wait for a table, maybe just talking local politics, fans mill three-deep at the ornate bar, which is back-lit to showcase five mirrored rows of bottles.

Framing the entry, mug shots of celeb diners offer grinning testimony to the popularity of the hangout. Beyond the host's podium stretches a long, narrow room boasting lots of dark wood, low booths upholstered in good-old-boy tones of leatherette, and dual rows of tables dressed in their business suits of white. Waitresses, themselves clad in retro black uniforms topped with starched white aprons, are lifers, likely as not to call you "hon" as they take your cocktail order. (You'll get the same pro service if you're seated in the "new" room to the right—not so new, after all these years—which doesn't quite deliver the same clublike charisma nor eye-of-the-hurricane bustle as the vintage original.)

The veteran servers will (wisely) counsel you to begin with the Mom-style chicken soup and chopped liver, both the best in town. In a nod to the 90s, the list of starters has been updated to include spicy Szechuan green beans and a lavosh-style pizza blooming with cilantro pesto. And seafood fettuccine leads a list of pastas the kitchen's learned to produce.

But if you're decidedly hungry, let yourself be steered to the lineup of steaks and pork chops; they're served with salad and a choice of potato. Otherwise, flip to the back cover of the menu for the Monte's signature classics like the Billy Reed Caesar burger, a real, old-time burger with a side of that celebrated salad; a sandwich of slow-roasted sirloin au jus on pumpernickel; or the same revered steak sandwich that was served for 48 years in Charlie's Café before its demise. The lunch crowd and late-night diners are allotted additional options, ranging from a classic Reuben to a meatloaf sandwich.

The wine list is here as a service, but beer or cocktails are the real order of the day.

MORTON'S, THE STEAKHOUSE

Gaviidae Common II, 555 Nicollet Mall, Minneapolis
(612) 673-9700 • mortons.com
$$$$; valet parking

WHEN IT COMES TO GREAT BEEF and plenty of it, this is the city of the three M's: Manny's, Murray's, and Morton's. Okay, Morton's, in contrast to its companion temples of steak worship, is not homegrown; it's from Chicago. But in the wide-open spaces of the Midwest that's almost considered home, so this "outsider" has been embraced like close kin.

What adds to its allure is the quasi-speakeasy atmosphere. Although there's no password required (if there were, it might be "Arnie [Morton] sent me"), you scurry in a small door, then descend a lengthy staircase to reach the grotto, where you'll be sequestered for the night.

The ceilings are low, the tables are compactly spaced, and the booths are meant for eyeing the glitterati of the night who make Morton's their club of choice. And the kitchen's firing line is open to view here, where they sell the sizzle as well as the steak. It's manned by gents who know their meat.

Expect portions even Paul Bunyan would be challenged to finish. The tone is set by displays of wine in mammoth bottles, log-sized spears of asparagus, tomatoes as big as bowling balls, and such. In practice, the side dishes to which those vegetables contribute are meant for sharing. And several steaks also come in what Morton's dubs "slightly smaller" sizes.

The double porterhouse for two, carved tableside, is the kitchen's showpiece, flanked by prime rib, filet mignon, New York strip, and rib eye of beef, as well as veal and lamb chops, a few token fish, and a mammoth lobster. To start, steakhouse classics abound: shrimp cocktail, crab cakes, and smoked salmon, as well as the consummate steakhouse salad of beefsteak tomatoes and onions among the list of greens. Vegetables follow the same classic steakhouse tradition: creamed spinach, jumbo asparagus, sautéed mushrooms, and potatoes—baked, hash browns, or lyonnaise-style.

Those who have merely dabbled may have room for dessert. Again, Morton's remains loyal to the tried and true: cheesecake, key lime pie, apple pie, soufflés baked to order—plus an innovative Godiva hot-chocolate cake.

Servers toe the fine line between discreet aloofness and warm, friendly bantering, sensing the mood of each party.

MURRAY'S

28 South Sixth Street
(612) 339-0909 • www.murraysrestaurant.com
$$$$; valet parking

WHO DIDN'T EAT HERE? The diners' hall of fame for Murray's includes almost every sports hero, film star, and politician who made their way to Minneapolis, along with a half-century of average Minnesota Joes and Janes who came for birthday and anniversary celebrations. On a recent Saturday, when every one of the 180 faux-Louis chairs were taken, a silver-haired couple toasted their 50th wedding anniversary while at the next table a Gen Xer with a buzz cut proposed to his girl.

Murray's operates in the same downtown location where it's been since 1946, with the familiar lacy red neon sign spelling out the family name for three generations. The restaurant is now in the able hands of founder Pat Murray's grandson, Tim. The recipes of Pat Murray's wife, Marie, are still kept under lock and key, and only the family is privy to the secret behind the supper club's legendary garlic toast, Caesar salad dressing, and steak seasoning. Career waitresses, primped in professional black outfits topped by crisp white aprons, have trod the floor for, well, forever, delivering that famous house garlic toast and making every single diner feel like a VIP. And if Murray's ever changed the décor, there'd be a stampede.

The room is a valentine in pink, with elaborate baroque mirrors, fancy drapes, and elegant chandeliers. Peek past the mirrored pillars through the sea of tables and you'll spot the petite stage in the rear, where a piano or violin reminisce, as they have for years. Everything about the place is classic, from the accolades framed in the foyer to the shadowy bar at the entrance, not to mention the time-honored menu.

Think Murray's and you think beef—big beef. This is the home of the Silver Butter Knife Steak, which deserves those capital letters. An order for two is carved tableside; from then on, that little silver butter knife is all it takes for guests to slice away. Even more elite are the Chateaubriand and the porterhouse (four pounds for three diners), for those who've won the lottery and believe there's no tomorrow. The not-insignificant price tag includes Murray's Caesar salad and a choice of potato (au gratin wins the vote) or fresh vegetable.

Appetizers are steakhouse classics: shrimp cocktail, stuffed mushrooms, crab cakes, oysters on the half-shell, baked brie. These days a few newcomers have made the list, including a walleye-and-wild-rice spring roll and a carpaccio of beef tenderloin. It's carved from the same top-drawer beef that's hung in Murray's locker to age a full 28 days so it becomes tender and takes on its special flavor.

Adding a horseradish-blue cheese crust is a fine way to gild this ruddy lily. And an order of béarnaise won't go wanting. Smaller cuts of beef also are listed à la carte. For those who think in terms of fish, the kitchen deftly prepares broiled walleye (Minnesota's state fish), salmon, or tuna.

The wine list rivals a telephone book in heft, with selections for the connoisseur (a wealthy one, anyway) backed by a strong suit in cabernet sauvignon.

No one has tampered with the dessert list for decades (well, except that now the orange sherbet is called "sorbet"). The kitchen's famed lemon icebox pie is the top seller, and for good reason. After that, when owner Tim wanders by to ask, "How's everything?" all one can muster is a purr.

NEW DELHI

1400 Nicollet Avenue South, Minneapolis
(612) 813-0000 • www.newdelhimn.com
$$; P

NEW DELHI IS FAR CLOSER to Delhi, its namesake, than many another Indian café in Minnesota. The others are, in fact, just that—cafés, and some mighty good ones among them. This spot earns its status as a restaurant.

No, you don't need a silk cravat or a little Chanel number to feel at home here—as a matter of fact, the diversity of the pleased clientele reflects the melting pot of India's capital itself. But fancy duds would not be out of place either. The low, latticed ceiling is draped with swoops of colorful silk saris. Bronzed pillars give the room a stately air, and dreamy wall murals celebrate the subcontinent's Mughal culture, which rose to its height five centuries ago. Hammered copper charger plates line neat rows of tables, crisply outfitted in white. Servers prove as polished as the cutlery.

New Delhi's triumvirate of owners became acquainted while working at the now-shuttered Chutney Bistro. (They've since added a New Delhi Bistro in Edina.) Instead of having an encyclopedic menu, the list concentrates on complex flavors rather than a uniform approach to seasoning. Punjabi, Parsi, and hot Goan dishes make an appearance in the lineup of entrées, which include lamb, chicken, and fish from clay tandoor ovens.

Among the tasty appetizers, the customary pastry packets of samosas and pakoras lead the way, featured singly or in enticing combination plates. If you're in the mood for soup, choose from sweet coconut, rich lentil, or lightly sour and spicy tomato. And save room for the array of flatbreads warm from the tandoor—naan, scented with garlic, onion, or coconut, and paratha, its whole-wheat cousin, stuffed with vegetables or chicken.

Entrées range from kabobs of sweet and gentle chicken tikka to a bold and fiery vindaloo perfumed with onions, tamarind, and garlic. Curry rules, as does korma, just as rich with herbs and spices. Each is prepared to the heat level requested with a choice of protein—chicken, lamb, goat, shrimp, fish, or, for a special treat, lobster.

Vegetarians fare even better, with a myriad of savory, well-spiced offerings ranging from eggplant paired with potatoes to a mélange of cauliflower, potatoes, and green peas; a medley of spinach and garbanzo beans; and veggies with lentils in coconut sauce or dancing with a touch of ginger. Paneer, the house-made cheese, works its way into many aromatic preparations. For an added fillip of flavor, the kitchen sends out tastes of its chutneys, both tamarind and mint.

27

India's traditional desserts make their appearance. The rice pudding is syrupy and creamy, while ras malai—the Indian version of cheesecake—and mango kulfi, a textured "ice cream," reward an open mind (and palate).

New Delhi serves those classic Indian beers named after bird life, as well as wines and cocktails. It's also fun to explore soft drinks such as the fruity mango shake or sweet or salty yogurt lassi.

NOCHEE

500 South Washington Avenue, Minneapolis
(612) 344-7000 • nochee.com
$$; P; M

FOR YEARS—decades—they couldn't give away this location along the tracks bordering the long-vacant train station in downtown Minneapolis. Now, as condos bloom around it and the Guthrie Theater has signed on as a near neighbor, it's the hottest spot within miles, especially as evenings segue from the dinner hour to late-late. In summer 2004 Nochee was born from the same local partnership behind La Bodega, Arezzo, and a couple of other pleasant but less ambitious bistros. It's a sleek temple of uber-sophistication, featuring a cool décor and menu and a parade of polished metrosexuals who call it home.

A compact function room at the street entrance makes you almost wish you had a meeting to attend. It beckons with a stylish look of steel gray and silver, overseen by a nearly life-sized papier-mâché horse suspended above the tables (which, in fact, serve regular diners after 10 o'clock, when the music takes over and the long, svelte, backlit bar begins to throb with mingling singles). A glassed-in wine tower sends the message that vino is taken seriously here—a message borne out by the inviting wine list of uncommon global labels. The soaring, shadowy, pewter-tinted walls are punctuated with provocative fixtures—call them artworks, maybe—that evoke a smile.

On the patio, a guitarist strums flamenco rhythms and a Spanish dancer yields to their seductive beat. The pair moves indoors in nippy weather, close to the matte black tabletops that are studies in chic simplicity.

That description fits the menu, too. The list of small plates alone could dispel dining boredom for a long time. No big tricks here, simply well-crafted renditions of some Med-Asian classics: beef carpaccio draped with Parmesan and Tuscan olive oil, the way it's meant to be; red snapper seviche with a bit of a South American kick; a bowl of mussels, clams, and shrimp simmered in a red curry broth that hints of Singapore; Szechuan-style back ribs with jalapeno corn bread; silky tuna tartare beside wasabi livened with crème fraiche, sake, and roe—well, you get the idea. Many of these pleasers reappear on the bar and late-night menus, too.

Three variations of risotto and a trio of pastas precede more hearty entrées, such as ruddy slices of Icelandic salmon strewn over a saffron and green pea risotto; halibut paired with a lively chorizo hash; beef tenderloin topped with ripe and creamy Gorgonzola and portobello mushrooms; and the wild card, a curry and potato cioppino that sneaks bold new flavors into the San Francisco fish stew.

Servers are affable and well informed; they chat, or don't, as your mood dictates. And pace the courses accordingly: the couple with the baby is in and out at cyclonic speed, while the romantic duo is free to linger in the shadows—well, at least till the music starts humming at ten. Then I dare anyone not to start tapping their feet.

OCEANAIRE SEAFOOD ROOM

Hyatt Regency Hotel, 1300 Nicollet Mall, Minneapolis
(612) 333-BASS • savvydiner.com
$$$$

THE OCEANAIRE IS TO SEAFOOD what Manny's is to steak—in other words, pretty darn primo. No surprise, because they're owned by the same local corporation and stand across the corridor from each other in the Hyatt Regency Hotel. Following the current steakhouse mode, every item here is ordered à la carte, and every portion is supersized.

The Oceanaire is designed, with a hint of tongue-in-cheek, to resemble the grand dining room of a classic ocean liner of the 30s—a clubby setting of burnished wood, gleaming metal, and sleek Deco lines. Even the menu's typeface looks oh-so-moderne.

But the oyster bar at the entrance is a paean to today's tastes and love of action. It lists eight varieties available at any given moment, shucked to order with a side of lively patter from the showman-oysterman.

From a roll call of over two dozen possible varieties of fish, snappy, informed servers sing off what's available this evening. The dozen-or-so species du jour are guaranteed fresh as they come, air-freighted from both coasts twice daily. Hawaiian opah, Florida grouper, North Atlantic cod, Canadian walleye,

Chilean sea bass, and Pacific swordfish are among the regulars. Diners may order this bounty simply grilled or broiled, served naked save for a spritz of olive oil and lemon. Or they can ask the chef to showcase his special treatments, such as sea bass with bacon-wilted spinach, horseradish, and brown butter or yellowfin tuna in a red wine reduction with exotic mushrooms. Live lobsters? You betcha. And weighing in at anywhere from 2 to 11 pounds, these guys aren't shrimps.

All menu add-ons are served in sharing-sized portions. Starters range from simple house-cured salmon and shrimp cocktail to retro throwbacks such as oysters Rockefeller and clams casino. The kitchen also produces the best crab cakes in town. The salad list honors all the classics, from Caesar to a wedge of iceberg. A couple of sides for the table are a good idea. Choose from buttermilk mashed potatoes or the kitchen's justly famous hash browns, asparagus with hollandaise, green beans amandine, or creamed corn (well, we promised "retro"). For those who can't abide something from the sea, there's a token list labeled "not seafood" that includes chicken, pork chops, and filet mignon.

It's not required to clean your plate here in order to qualify for dessert. (In fact, the doggie bags are as classy a status symbol as sacks from Neiman Marcus.) Again, order one for the entire table, choosing a baked Alaska (straight from that 30s cruise ship), cheesecake with fresh berries, a chocolate turtle cake, and more.

The Oceanaire's wine list does the trick, but you almost yearn to be sipping a martini in case Fred and Ginger sweep through the room. And if not, the celebrity artists at nearby Orchestra Hall may well show up for an after-concert supper.

ORIGAMI

30 North First Street, Minneapolis
(612) 333-8430 • origamirestaurant.com
$$–$$$

WORDS LIKE "AWESOME" and "best in flyover land" regularly float from the lips of sushi aficionados as they finally leave the place after one last ("Last! I promise!") morsel, a little lighter in the pocketbook but with smiles of contentment on their faces. They're also mighty pleased they'd finally snagged a coveted spot in the elegantly restored Warehouse District storefront, which offers only two slim rows of seats and a curvy sushi bar in the rear.

Behind the sushi bar, the black belts of the profession—well, black aprons, in this case—ply their craft, deftly slicing up what fans claim is the freshest sushi in these landlocked parts and affixing the tasty tidbits to plump pillows of sticky rice before patrons' transfixed eyes. The variations are myriad, from akagi (red clam) to uni (sea urchin), with scallop, squid, salmon, tuna, snapper, oyster, sea bass, and eel—and that's just for starters. The maki rolls also number in the dozens, including a couple concocted to delight vegetarian diners.

Modern artwork (including origami birds) adorns the walls of creamy exposed brick. The closely packed, glass-topped tables are set with tasteful simplicity, with crisp white tablecloths, chopsticks, and a single votive candle. The room is lit by pin spots affixed to the high ceiling, the better to see and be seen in this gathering place for the "in" crowd in the arts and dining world (joined by bus drivers, office temps, and chefs from other establishments on their days off, a testimony to the broad appeal of supreme sushi).

There's life, for those who crave it, beyond nigiri and sashimi. A select list of Asian nibbles offers tempura, gyoza (dumplings), Origami's style of wontons jauntily garnished with baubles of flying fish roe, and a seaweed salad laced with sesame oil and ponzu sauce. In addition, several vegetable dishes, celebrating eggplant, spinach, mushrooms, or asparagus, often prove to be the sleepers of the evening.

The habitués in basic black sip warm sake with their hamachi (yellowfin) and caterpillar rolls (eel wrapped in avocado), but beer and martinis also suit the menu well and have found a following.

Origami has opened a second location in Minnetonka's Ridgedale Mall; it's the same primo sushi and adept chefs but, most agree, less atmospheric.

PALOMINO

825 Hennepin Avenue, Mineapolis
(612) 339-3800 • r-u-i.com
$$–$$$; P

IS THAT *THE* MATISSE of gamboling nudes? And how about that matching wall-sized still life? Ooh, and the geometric mural's surely a Picasso? Well, maybe not, but the repros set the tone of lighthearted whimsy that prevails here, running from the ceiling's undulating moldings in café au lait and claret to the futuristic art-glass lighting.

Yes, Palomino is a place to enjoy the see-and-be-seen scene from its closely packed tables on the second floor overlooking Hennepin Avenue's theater district. (In fact, a three-course pretheater menu is offered at exceptional value.) Suits dominate the down-to-business lunch trade, while evenings draw a pleasant mix of patrons fueling up for arts events (including the occasional Broadway star who's performing) and couples hooking up with friends for a night on the town.

A stroll past Palomino's extensive open kitchen at the entrance offers show-and-tell evidence of what's hot—literally—on the evening's menu. Coals glow in the wood-fired pizza oven and the hearth where meats are spit-roasted. Braids of garlic and displays of fancy oils, olives, and pepperoncini convey the Italianate flavor that informs this stylish rotisserie.

Servers garbed in silky, smoke-blue shirts are swift to deliver the crusty Tuscan bread that starts the meal, accompanied by a tasty tomato compote. Starters meant for sharing include crisped calamari with garlic aioli, a suave Dungeness crab and artichoke dip, and oven-roasted clams and mussels. Or subdivide a thin-crust pizza with close to a dozen choices of embellishments. Salads range from Greek, chop-chop, and Caesar to a blue cheese and hazelnut creation that incorporates tasty bits of bacon.

Decision-making gets no easier when it comes to the tempting list of entrées. Seafood fares well here, as in king salmon presented with artichoke tartar sauce and raspberry-infused wild greens, served with polenta, Gorgonzola, and roasted corn relish—a seasonal hit, as is the marlin with French lavender butter and fire-roasted veggies. Chicken appears in four treatments but, let's face it, folks come here for more substantial meat. The lamb shank with risotto fills the bill, as does the spit-roasted pork loin, served with rhubarb confit and Parmesan mashed russets. Those who swear by beef aren't disappointed in the kitchen's signature New York strip, served with fries and a choice of tempting sauces.

That leaves pasta, and these lusty plates prove equally satisfying. Oven-baked penne, a rustic favorite, competes with noodles in tosses such as Gorgonzola, hazelnuts, and cracked pepper or an Alfredo spiffed up with pan-seared prawns and scallops. Yes, there's even a classic spaghetti-and-meatballs offering on the menu for those who swear by Neapolitan tradition. Mercifully, all pastas may be ordered in starter sizes for those dying to taste those roasted viands as well.

Desserts don't stray into the realm of untried surprises—instead, there's an archetypical tiramisu, crème brûlée, cheesecake, and a molten chocolate cake that's de rigueur. There's always a seasonal fruit cobbler as well.

The coffee's as good as you hoped for—the Torrefazione roasters' work from Italy. Choose draft beer from American microbreweries or fairly priced wine from an international selection. Or repair to the lounge at the entrance and settle into a comfy chair to complete your census of Hennepin's passersby over an after-dinner snifter.

PETER'S GRILL

114 South Eighth Street, Minneapolis
(612) 333-1981 • petersgrill.com
$; no alcohol

SOME INSTITUTIONS NEVER CHANGE, and you can thank your lucky stars that Peter's is among them. If ever it were to shut its doors—don't panic, not gonna happen—the Smithsonian would no doubt be there in a Washington minute, ready to preserve it as a shrine.

It claims to be the oldest restaurant in Minneapolis, serving up plain, nononsense home cooking ever since 1914. That's the pivotal year in Minnesota history when Peter Atcas, a young Greek immigrant, shut down his fruit stand to take on bigger things. These days the café is run by his nephews, Peter and Andy Atsidakas, who also hail from Greece. They know better than to tamper with their uncle's formula for success: "Good honest food, a lot of food, and good prices."

Those prices seem to have been frozen back in the 30s, when the café took on its present art moderne look, as best personified in the iconic logo of a pert young waitress in a frilly starched cap and apron holding up a heaping platter. The Deco lamps still dangle from the ceiling above dark booths that line the windows and circle the terrazzo floor. While the booths are reserved for larger parties, single patrons do call this place home. Peter's draws many, many solo regulars from the surrounding office towers who sneak in a hearty breakfast before beginning the day or grab a stool at the pair of U-shaped diner counters for reliably nutritious fare that hasn't changed for decades. Those who don't mind eating early are just as likely to return for dinner before the doors are locked promptly at 7:45 p.m.

Those dinners, at giveaway prices, feature soup or tomato juice, cole slaw or tossed salad, choice of potato, and a homemade roll, along with enough ribs, chicken, meatloaf, or roast turkey to feed a football team—all for five dollars, give or take a few pennies. But don't forget to heed the graying sign in the window that indicates "It's Apple Pie Time" and indulge in a juicy slice of the homemade favorite. All Peter's desserts are homemade, so don't overlook the chocolate cake, either.

Career waitresses, who today have traded in 30s uniforms for shirts of forest green, probably turn most of their tip money over to the podiatrist, for they've tramped the terrazzo in double-time for years and years. Count on these pros to deliver lunch orders with proper speed and accuracy, with not a minute to lose in the "Hi, I'm Shirley and I'll be your server" game. Instead, it's armloads of crockery plates loaded with three-decker clubhouses or giant sandwiches of corned beef, baked ham, sliced turkey, or chopped liver, preceded by vegetable soup from a recipe that never falters. Others swear by the burgers on homemade buns, served, retro-style, with cottage cheese and peaches or—with a nod to the twenty-first century—with fries and slaw.

People eking out pensions come here; so do postal workers from the office next door; so do the nearby banks' accountants, who know a good deal when they see it; and so did President Clinton, in 1994, when he ordered a Canadian bacon and egg sandwich on pumpernickel with vegetable soup, apple pie, and diet Coke and wrote Peter a swell thank-you tribute for it—a note that now honors each menu.

SAPOR

428 Washington Avenue North, Minneapolis
(612) 375-1971 • saporcafe.com
$$; P; O

THE BIG QUESTION: Will diners stray this far north of the bright lights of downtown? Even when the street is closed for road construction all summer long? Admittedly, it was tough going at first for Sapor when it opened back in 2000 on the far northern fringe of the city's Warehouse District, with no passersby at night. But it survived its once-inaccessible location, and by now the condo craze has reached the neighborhood. As buildings were restored and two-income couples moved this way, they craved someplace close to home to eat. Sapor fills the bill. And because of adjacent parking, the business lunch trade is mighty brisk, too.

Housed on the first floor of one of those behemoth brick warehouses, Sapor wears a cool, clean, and unassuming look—blond wood tables, walls patterned in chocolate and café au lait that showcase local art, simple warehouse lights, and well-spaced seating. The setting is as discreet and neutral as a business suit, but the food is not.

Co-owners Julie Steenerson and Tanya Siebenaler, who also serves as chef, believe in supporting sustainable farming, and they honor their purveyors on seasonally changing menus. The proof is in the pudding, as they say. Highlights include heirloom tomatoes served as a late-summer starter, sided with a ricotta-basil fritter and dashed with balsamic vinaigrette; a sopapilla of slow-cooked pork (give Fischer's Purebred Hog Farm in Waseca the credit), and a takeoff on the sweet Spanish fritter, here turned savory, served with honey chili sauce and sweet corn salsa, another star of the appetizer list. The sesame-crusted calamari, some of the lightest in town, are enhanced by a topping of roasted carrot slivers spiked with ginger and green olives. The globally inspired soups succeed as well.

A half-dozen entrées and perhaps a nightly special form the corps of the menu. Sapor's signature dish is the miso-baked wild salmon, served with a frisky wasabi potato cake, gingered vegetables, and peanuts. Close behind in popularity is the rib eye of beef, accompanied by a purple potato gratin and onions braised in Champagne grapes. Cannelloni, stuffed with roasted red peppers and local goat cheese, pleases more than vegetarians, so fair warning: It's often sold out.

For desserts, the decided hit is a chocolate-coffee crème brûlée served with chocolate chip cookies. Coffee? Of course. Café con leche, too. And a small but diverse wine list with a dozen or so interesting, value-forward options by the glass adds to the pleasure of the evening. Servers are quick to suggest personal favorites, and their advice is worth a listen. They're adept at sensing a party's temperament and pacing a meal to suit one's mood.

SAWATDEE

607 South Washington Avenue, Minneapolis
(612) 338-6451 • sawatdee.com
$–$$
Seven additional locations

THE PATH FROM Supenn Harrison's native Thailand to a stellar string of Twin Cities Thai restaurants led her not only across the ocean but uphill. For a woman, and a foreigner, it wasn't always easy, as she now can acknowledge with a smile.

Her story begins in a hospital where she worked as a medical technician upon first coming to this country. Colleagues who became addicted to the fresh spring rolls she'd bring in as treats encouraged her to market them at the State Fair in 1976. That success prodded Supenn to make the leap and lease a tiny café on Lake Street. She named it Siam, and word spread fast about how good it was. She was off and running.

In 1983, she opened her first Sawatdee in downtown Saint Paul, adorned with gilded dragons, carved roof beams, delicate statuary from her homeland, and hangings of Thai silk. Next came what's now become her main location on the fringe of downtown Minneapolis, another museum piece of a café. Since then, tilting with what she calls the "good old guys" who may have thought a woman's place was in the kitchen but not to head an enterprise, she labored to secure the necessary bank loans to bring her tasty fare to the burbs. She now boasts eight locations.

"I was a pioneer in the field," she recalls with pride, introducing Midwestern palates to authentically seasoned dishes lush with cilantro, lemongrass, and lots of garlic. These days, diners get the message. Those original fresh spring rolls still take pride of place on her menus, served chilled with a rich peanut dipping sauce. Satays—little skewers of Thai-spiced pork or chicken—make another tasty nibble.

Som tam—a spicy salad of green papayas, peanuts, dried shrimp, and tomatoes anointed in fresh lemon juice—provides a zesty contrast to Supenn's suave version of her country's national culinary icon, pad Thai, that meal-in-itself noodle dish festooned with egg, crisp bean sprouts, scallions, peanuts, and a lemon wedge. Seafood is another forte here, livened with ginger, curry, and even potent jalapenos. Most stir-fries are easily adaptable—just select beef, chicken, shrimp, tofu, or mock duck, and it's tossed into the aromatic meld. Diners also can indicate the degree of heat these entrées may carry, from Minnesota-mild to South Asian-searing.

Jasmine rice attends most dishes, but when time rolls around for dessert, sticky rice is showcased, either with a Thai custard, enriched with coconut milk, or combined with slices of fresh mango. Supenn returns each year to Thailand to renew her spirit and refresh her palate, adding new menu items upon her return. But her original motto has never faltered: "Thai it, you'll like it." So true.

THE SKYROOM

Marshall Field's, 700 Nicollet Mall, Minneapolis
(612) 375-6936
$; lunch only; F

FOR MORE DECADES than most folks can remember, the SkyRoom has served as a magnet for lunchers from all walks of the cityscape. Located atop the prince of downtown department stores formerly known as Dayton's, the SkyRoom continues to draw shoppers in search of sustenance. You'll share the cafeteria line with office workers, execs in a hurry, retirees spending an afternoon downtown, and students on break between classes. In other words, it's become an institution, and rightfully so.

The twelfth-floor setting, blazing with daylight from the windows lining its perimeter, is all white and bright, with tile floors, Formica tables, and steel patio chairs, with curvy waves on the ceiling that mirror the flow of the salad bar below.

It's a role model for all salad bars, lined with composed salads to scoop up as well as fresh fixings to mix and match at whim, accented by a daily choice of three soups to complete a quick meal, including something to please its vegetarian clientele.

Behind the salad bar stretch a series of short-order counters for those who crave something hot or a bit heartier. Stop at the Deli for thick sandwiches, grilled or cold, a multitude of wraps, and kettles of soup, such as the legendary Minnesota wild rice recipe that Dayton's made famous and Marshall Field's has never seen fit to tamper with.

The Grill specializes in dogs, burgers, and fries, as well as more esoteric sausages, such as chicken andouille or a tequila-chicken link. The neighboring pizza counter serves its pies by the slice and also features signature pastas, including a toss of noodles with chicken and Gorgonzola, lemon penne, and a spicy Bolognese.

Those seeking a taste from south of the border lineup at the Tortilleria for black bean soup, taco salad, fish tacos, fajitas of all denominations, quesadillas, nachos, or a hefty barbecued pork burrito. The list goes on, but not the line, for these pros are adept at keeping things moving right along.

And the price is right.

SOLERA

900 Hennepin Avenue, Minneapolis
(612) 338-0062 • solera-restaurant.com
$$; valet parking; O

WHEN CHEF-OWNERS Tim McKee and Josh Thoma opened Solera in 2003, people wondered whether the boys could make it back in the bright lights of the big city. After all, everybody loved their La Belle Vie, which truly delivered "the good life" to small-town diners in Stillwater on the Minnesota River. Jessica Lange ate there, along with platinum cardholders from nearby Andersen Windows and 3M. The two were also alums of the prestigious D'Amico dining empire, which had produced such winners as D'Amico Cucina and Campiello.

The pair had proved they could truck their talents to a sleepy river town and make a spectacular go of things. So when they took over a failed location in downtown Minneapolis and announced an informal tapas concept, it was greeted like the Second Coming. So, it had better be good.

It is. Solera has been packed since its opening, aided by its spot in the heart of the theater district. But even when marquees are dark, there may be a wait for a table. Stick it out and Solera delivers, in the form of a menu of small plates—two dozen hot dishes and another couple dozen cold, all informed by the tapas-grazing concept the fellows researched in Spain.

To investigate their takes on the best of Barcelona, simply follow the whim of your palate or advice from the tour guide serving your table. They're sweethearts; rather than overselling the choices, they're more likely to caution you with a "Stop!" when the ordering gets out of hand.

The kitchen isn't into shocking your sensibilities. Instead, the food is based on comfort, quality, and value. While you're still scanning the menu, it sends out rounds of peasant bread painted with olive oil, lots of sweet and heady garlic, and sieved tomatoes: a taste of sun, a touch of Spain. Plates range from cocktail nibbles as light as olives or almonds to hearty rustic offerings such as earthy sausages, pork ribs, calamari, or bits of roasted rabbit. Proceed down the list till they finally turn off the lights.

Winners include Serrano ham, Spain's answer to prosciutto, curled around slim breadsticks topped with slivers of Manchego cheese. Salmon, lightly smoked, goes uptown with baubles of trout roe. The basic building blocks— shrimp, cheese, sausage, vegetables, and such—get flavor lifts with vinegar, herbs, and other surprise kickers, such as goat cheese fritters dipped in honey. And so it goes, from gazpacho to churros, the Spanish doughnuts doing duty as Solera's star dessert, served with an espresso cup of cinnamon-scented chocolate for dipping. Sherries and a Spanish wine list add to the experience.

The setting itself deserves a docent. It's a museum of modern art without the awe or attitude, composed of a labyrinth of small rooms swathed in dark, warm tones of plum and charcoal punctuated with provocative tiles and sculptures made expressly for the place. The bar at the entrance is equally inviting, with a communal table for singles that adds to the sizzle.

VINCENT

1100 Nicollet Mall, Minneapolis
(612) 630-1189 • vincentarestaurant.com
$$–$$$; valet parking

HIS NAME IN VINCENT, but pronounce it "Van-sont"—he's French to the core, and so is his menu. Young Vincent Francoual hopped a plane from his hometown in southern France to head to New York, where he made a name for himself in the kitchens of the prestigious Le Bernardin restaurant, known for its way with fish. But love brought him to Minnesota when he married a flight attendant based here. After wowing patrons of the former Café un deux trois, he took the plunge and opened his own eponymous bistro in a prime location on the Nicollet Mall, just paces from Orchestra Hall.

The space is lofty, clean-cut, and contemporary in feel, with a small bar on one side, where photos of Vincent's village brighten the walls, and a sizeable dining space on the other, lit with full-length corner windows.

Yes, that's Chef Vincent and crew at work in the back, spotted in the open-to-view kitchen. He often takes a nightly pause to circulate among his guests, beaming a Gallic smile that charms folks almost as much as his creative cooking.

He takes inspiration where he finds it rather than in the confines of a classic bistro kitchen. Yes, escargot appear in garlic butter, but the list also salutes a carpaccio of beets with whipped goat cheese, his signature starter, and celery root custard made with mushroom consommé and a brunoise of root vegetables. That appetizer list always includes what he calls "something strange but good"—a little stretch for some Minnesota palates, rewarded by dishes like braised tripe with garlic croustade, for example. The menu continues with what Vincent dubs a "not so hungry" number, a smaller portion of something tasty like scallops, leeks, and fingerling potatoes in orange sauce, or stuffed quail in port wine and a mushroom-squash ragout.

Entrées lead off with some of the fish dishes that have secured Vincent's reputation, such as fennel seed–crusted salmon with lobster-infused fennel and green pea risotto or New Zealand grouper served with shitake mushrooms, cipollini onions, cauliflower puree, and lemon confit. Daringly he'll pair wild boar ravioli with braised cabbage or fuse continents and toss spring lamb with Indian spices. And vegetarians always can count on a well-designed course of their own.

Vincent is one of the few fine-dining restaurants in town to offer a complex cheese course—works of art in their own right rather than mere slabs on a plate. For instance, Wisconsin chèvre sails out paired with a sun-dried tomato relish and fried parsnips. Desserts receive equal attention from the chef. Consider not one, but three elite creams on a single order: crème caramel, crème brûlée, and a petite pot de crème.

A new addition to the regular menu is Vincent's prix fixe bistro dinner, available weekdays, with courses that change three times weekly and often include a roulade of smoked salmon; roast beets and crème fraiche served on baby greens, with crisp Indian bread as a starter; and confit of duck leg paired with cauliflower, wild rice, and a sauce of cider vinegar and Dijon mustard.

Vincent's house wine is made by a boyhood friend from his region, a satisfying vin du table. The list includes many seldom-seen labels, too.

CHAPTER TWO

Northeast Minneapolis
and the University Area

BOBINO CAFÉ AND WINE BAR

222 East Hennepin Avenue, Minneapolis
(612) 623-3301 • bobino.com
$$; P; O

IF YOU BUILD IT, they will come, all right—in this case, across the river from downtown Minneapolis. Bobino was a trailblazer in luring serious diners to East Hennepin by establishing a snazzy little place to eat in this then-ungentrified, blue-collar neighborhood. It's reminiscent of a New York–style supper club, visited by couples with an eye to style as well as interesting wine and food. The message it sends is one of understated chic, conveyed by walls of blushing beige hung with a few choice modern paintings above blond wood floors and tabletops. A double-sided bar separates this dining room from a cozy, street-side bar area where wine enthusiasts gather (the full menu is available here as well).

Servers, buoyed both by enthusiasm and menu expertise, offer sound suggestions to the undecided on what's the best of the best of chef Jascon Schellin's current fare. Her list leads off with tiny bites to nibble over drinks, such as a plate of imported olives or tastes of cheese with fruit and nuts. Then it's on to the small plates, such as grilled scallops and parsnip roesti over warm frisee greens with almonds, grapefruit segments, and bacon vinaigrette, or hickory-smoked whitefish on a salad of oven-dried tomatoes drizzled with preserved-lemon crème fraiche. Salads on which to make a full meal also flourish, in the form of arugula tossed with fingerling potatoes, shaved red onion, tiny haricots verts, and a lightly poached egg or a generous plate of baby spinach joined by roasted pears, balsamic-steeped figs, crisped prosciutto, and hearty chunks of Stilton cheese.

A list of a half-dozen entrées inspires confidence that the kitchen is focusing on doing a few favorite dishes well. That's the case with a plate of pan-roasted monkfish wrapped in a shawl of prosciutto atop mustard greens; a vegetable napoleon build upon Parmesan polenta; or grilled Fisher Farms pork medallions plated with caraway-braised fennel, grilled radicchio, and crispy sweet potatoes.

A word about the wine list, and that word is *wonderful*. Bottles, including many open for tasting by the glass, come from lesser-known vintners of the New World, Old World, and Third World, offered at good value. In fact, Bobino has led the trend growing among smaller, interesting cafés of offering bottles at half price one night a week, a welcome incentive to experiment.

In summertime diners may make their way to the patio to catch the breeze and often catch a movie as well, played upon the brick façade. Bobino's founders also own the adjacent Starlight Lounge and Mojito, based in Saint Louis Park.

GARDENS OF SALONICA

19 Fifth Street NE, Minneapolis
(612) 378-0611
$; F

THESSALONIKI (A.K.A. SALONICA) is the hub of northeast Greece. Gardens of Salonica is a mainstay of northeast Minneapolis—certainly a striking parallel. Never mind that our local namesake is a bit less warm and sunny than its mother city, they're equally strong in—what's the Greek word for joie de vivre? You know: the reason Shirley Valentine left England.

Fancy, not at all. Gardens of Salonica is a typical taverna, with no effort wasted on frills like flowers on the tables—or even tablecloths, for heaven's sake—it's simply a warm, inviting storefront space. The bright, white walls, trimmed in Grecian blue, support an old-time pressed-tin ceiling. There's a stone fountain, a couple of abstract sculptures that invoke the art shop next door, and the plink of Greek bouzouki music wafting over the dozen-plus tables that populate this comfy café.

Nordeast's bounty of young artists eat here, as do potential backers in business suits, along with trades people in blue collars who know a good meal when they come across one. The prices are as favorable for repeat visits as the friendly service.

Honk if you love garlic. It's the star player in many, many of the appetizer dips. Tzatziki, born of smooth and creamy homemade yogurt blended with cucumbers, is perfect for spooning onto rounds of pita bread, as is the skordalia, a puree of potatoes brightened with a squeeze of lemon; the melitzana, a meaty puree of roasted eggplant and fava beans; and a puree of golden split peas. Steamed beet greens, artichoke hearts bathed in olive oil and lemon, and octopus swimming in vinaigrette also compete for attention as starters. The best bet is to summon the combination plate, which includes samplings of three of your choice.

Entrées include soup or a Greek salad, complete with crumbles of feta and a sprinkling of kalamata olives. Other familiar choices include pastitsio, a close cousin of the quintessential "hot dish" favored by Minnesotans, and dolmades constructed of grape leaves wrapped around seasoned rice.

Gardens of Salonica presents one of the best versions in town of moussaka, eggplant and an aromatic meat sauce under a frosting of béchamel. Share that and a lamb dish, such as gyros, souvlaki, or stew with orzo pasta in red sauce, and life starts looking pretty good.

Vegetarians easily become addicted to the phyllo-wrapped pastries filled with one's choice of spinach, mushrooms, a leek-lemon-garlic trio, or feta and ricotta. Add a bowl of avgolemono soup and dinner is complete.

Well, almost. Let's not forget dessert. Again, crisp leaves of hand-wrapped phyllo harbor tasty fillings such as lemon or apricot cream, a rich custard bathed in syrup, a quintessential baklava enriched with three varieties of nuts, and a heady chocolate-hazelnut composition splashed with brandy. Or take the higher road with poached figs or a yogurt sundae.

Wine is served, taverna-style, in sturdy juice glasses. Greek labels and beer are offered, tempered with listings from America. Just as addictive is the heady Greek coffee, served in a demitasse and thick enough to savor with a spoon. In summer, it's poured over shaved ice, dubbed a frappe, and sent out to save patrons from the Minnesota heat.

JAX CAFÉ

1928 University Avenue NE, Minneapolis
(612) 789-7297 • jaxcafe.com
$$; P; O; F

IN 1910 STAN KOZLAK erected a brick building to house his various businesses serving the blue-collar Polish neighborhood fondly called Nordeast. It was converted to Jax Café (named for the popular New Orleans beer) in 1933—the moment prohibition ended—and its grand mahogany bar has been a monument to Northeast Minneapolis's hospitality ever since.

Joe Kozlak, the eldest of Stan's five boys, expanded the business in 1943 as his own family expanded. Today it's run by his grandkids, since Joe's son Bill Kozlak and his wife, Ruth, recently retired after decades of serving as welcoming icons at the host's post. Today their son's practiced eye roves the premises. The restaurant features a series of comfortable, wood-paneled dining rooms and the garden patio beyond with a slowly turning millwheel, waterfall, and trout stream, where guests vie to net their own dinners and pose for photos on the banks. For many a Minneapolis resident, the opening of the patio and first trout dinner signal that it's truly spring.

Other seafood varieties, including the lobsters in the bar's aquarium, are flown in with regularity. Minnesota walleyed pike is nearly as popular as the aged and cut-to-order tenderloins and New York strips upon which Jax has staked its reputation. Salmon, scallops in a garlic cream sauce, and jumbo shrimp round out the seaside menu, abetted by nightly specials like Carolina smoked fish cakes. Or halibut verde, humming with a spicy tomatillo salsa. But to be honest, many a diner comes here for red meat.

"Famous for steaks," the menu boasts, and they aren't kidding. The tender prime rib with a sassy side of horseradish sauce is a best seller, followed closely by the well-aged tenderloin, the New York strip, and the 24-ounce porterhouse (for those whose eyes are bigger than their stomachs). And if you've had a hard time lately finding vintage emblems of haute cuisine like chicken Kiev or a pastry-wrapped Wellington on a menu, this is the place to satisfy your yearnings.

Classic supper-club fare like shrimp cocktail, oysters, herring, and stuffed mushrooms lead the appetizer list, but tasty updates have sneaked their way onto the menu, too, in the form of artichoke dip and cilantro crab cakes. Save room for Jax's famous clam chowder or the perky house salad that accompanies all entrées.

It's always been a place for celebrations— Mother's Day, New Year's Eve, high school proms, and football lunches. Kids Bill once lifted into highchairs now return with children of their own. Birthday cakes appear with regularity from the kitchen, with a few more candles as the years go by. Couples return to celebrate their 50th wedding anniversary here in the hall where they held their wedding dance. "Lots of people get engaged at these tables and come back to get married in the patio," Bill reminisces. The numerous framed awards on the restaurant's walls stand as testimonials to Jax's reliably fine food, and the Kozlak family underscores that bonus with enduring hospitality.

KAFE 421

421 14th Avenue SE, Minneapolis
(612) 623-4900 • kafe421.com
$–$$; P

DINING NEAR THE UNIVERSITY of Minnesota campus got a whole lot more pleasant early in 2004 as folks—more professors than students, though a lively seasoning of both, plus devoted parents and their friends—discovered Kafe 421.

Passing by the new little entry on the university scene, it appears to be your typical student eatery, turning out fast food to go for ravenous kids on the move. But simply let on that you'd like to dine in, and Georgia, the gracious and accomplished host-proprietor, will lead you to a back room off the street to settle down. Lively walls in tones of persimmon and posters of Greece (Georgia's

EMILY'S LEBANESE DELI

641 University Avenue NE • Minneapolis • (612) 379-4069

Smack in the middle of this Polish Northeast neighborhood, Emily's introduced the city to the delights of Middle Eastern eats. For decades, the unassuming, monochromatic setting has served as Mecca for minty tabouleh, superior kibbeh, and a range of traditional homemade dips, salads, and meat dishes fashioned from family recipes. They're displayed in the deli case in the rear, ready to take out or eat in, as many lively parties seem to choose.

native land) accent her pan-Mediterranean menu, which also tips a cap to the fare Georgia has found to be most popular at her former south Minneapolis place, The Best Steakhouse, as well as the more sophisticated dishes developed over her longtime career as a caterer.

At noon, choose from salads, sandwiches, and pastas that exceed the ordinary. After dusk there's time to linger over full-course meals. Georgia's lemon-infused grape leaves prove more refined than those of many an Athenian taverna, served warm with a touch of yogurt-cucumber sauce. They're light on garlic, as is her hummus, but the eggplant dip makes up for any lack that fans of the stinking bulb may notice.

The kitchen's Greek salad elevates the customary toss with its thoughtful presentation, topped with pungent chunks of feta and pale green peppers in a suave, subtle update of the islands' dressing. Here, too, the spanakopita (phyllo-crusted squares of spinach pie) is sent out on a dainty bed of greens, a touch that escalates it to a mini-meal.

Some swear the lamb shank is the best in town, tender and laced with flavor, presented upon a winsome triple-tomato risotto. It's big enough to share, and then some. So is the café's pork chop, husky and full-flavored in a Merlot sauce, with whipped potatoes that catch every drop.

Typical Greek pastries are listed, but they prove lighter—okay, classier—than those customary oversweet temptations. There's also an addictive chocolate number that defies willpower as well as national origin.

Greek wines are available but are not always the best choice on the eclectic list. Not only does Georgia serve Greek coffee, she's been known to instruct guests in the entire ceremony, another gracious touch.

LORING PASTA BAR

327 14th Avenue SE, Minneapolis
(612) 378-4849 • loringcafe.com
$$; valet parking; O; M

MINNEAPOLIS CAN BOAST its share of landmarks by high-profile architects—
I. M. Pei, Philip Johnson, Frank Gehry . . . and Jason McLean.

Mc-who? Okay, so he didn't go to architecture school. He was schooled, instead, in theater as a young actor. Yet, once he found his true calling, his self-designed cafés became the envy of many restaurateurs, who'd donate their first-born to learn the secret of McLean's success. Well, here it is: pure magic, according to the evidence of this dramatic venue in the University of Minnesota's Dinkytown. The man understands, like no one else, that dining is more than mere calories. It's an escape into an illusion.

And the Loring Pasta Bar is fairyland. Having risen from the figurative ashes of a former campus icon, Gray's Drugs, it's a bistro straight from La Boheme—Paris as it was meant to be—or perhaps even *A Midsummer Night's Dream* in Minnesota.

Exposed beams hover in the ceiling, two stories above the floor tiles. There are antique exposed bricks and French windows that open onto the sidewalk, where greenery is set amid the seats. Tiny trees and twinkle lights punctuate the indoor sea of tables (there isn't a bad one in the room) with a view of the open kitchen and the gazebo-like stage where musicians make certain you fall in love.

The servers are probably actors in the making—at least, Jason clearly encourages them to be. Piercings outnumber nametags, just like in the golden days of the original, still mourned, Loring Café, which succumbed to a landlord's grievance in 2001. The open kitchen is part of the conviction that the hired hands are people, too, as much a political statement as a design trend. —*Hello*, these people make the food you're enjoying, and they in turn get instant feedback by observing diners' pleased reactions.

Ah, the food. Longtime Loring fans have welcomed the revival of several of Jason's kitchen classics: the artichoke ramekin, a legend in its own time and copied by many a wannabe since, or the gutsy Caesar salad and the classy pizzas with tender, fragile crusts.

The asparagus appetizer is another sure winner; calling it a salad is like calling foie gras "liver." Pastas vary in intrigue from staid to extra-special, but count on your server to offer a candid opinion. Penne, laced with crimini mushrooms, pine nuts, raisins, and rosemary, gets a near-unanimous thumbs up. So does the walleye on the entrée list, and no one does our state fish justice like

SURDYK'S CHEESE SHOP

303 East Hennepin Avenue • (612) 379-9757 • www.surdyks.com

This is the mothership. For the cities' dedicated cheese lovers, Surdyk's is as good as it gets, with over 300 varieties imported from a dozen countries from which to choose, including 29 varieties of blue cheese, 12 variations of brie, 11 goat cheeses, and the list goes on. Fresh cheeses flourish here, too, in the form of ricotta, mascarpone, quark, and more. And because the shop does such high-volume business, turnover is quick, which guarantees that the cheese you're sent home with is as fresh as a sailor's remarks.

The staff is intimately acquainted with the nuances of what's in the display cases and genially dispenses knowledge and advice (including wine pairings) along with generous samples. The shop's deli also features all the go-with items to please your party or picnic guests. And, of course, there are thousands of bottles of wine and spirits right next door.

this kitchen, brushing it with a pecan-maple sauce and placing it with native-grown wild rice. Lamb chops in a mustard rub are married to garlic mashed potatoes and a tomato-mint demi-glace to complete the plate. At this café Jason has added a couple of steaks for those who must have them. Best deal: Round up a couple of friends and order the four-course platter, served family-style for four or more people. There's a lovely, affordable wine list, too.

Despite its frat-house location, the Loring Pasta Bar is not primarily a venue for students, unless they're working on a Ph.D. in hospitality. Expect, instead, the neighborhood profs as well as arts-scene habitués from all over the metro. For a slightly different but no less magical dining experience courtesy of Jason, wander a few paces down the street to the legendary Varsity Theater where this entrepreneur has worked his customary wonder and now offers a drink-and-dine cabaret experience.

MODERN CAFÉ

337 13th Avenue NE, Minneapolis
(612) 378-9882
$$

MODERN INDEED! Well, it may have been, back in 1940. Since then, time has stood still in this Nordeast café, reclaimed (but not modernized in appearance) by talented chef-owner Jim Grell. He saw the potential in this longtime greasy spoon, signed the papers, and started putting his own quirky twists on its comfort food. The décor is as spare as ever—hanging "schoolroom" lights shining down on well-worn linoleum tiles of maroon and gray and bare beige walls (except for a mounted swordfish—who knows why?—above the soda counter). But these days the vintage high-backed wooden booths, counter stools, and scatter-

KRAMARCZUK'S DELI

215 East Hennepin Avenue • Minneapolis • (612) 379-3018

Kramarczuk's isn't simply a meat market, it's a way of life. The Ukrainian owners who made their way here after fleeing tough times in their homeland opened the market decades ago to serve this Northeast neighborhood. In gratitude for their new citizenship, they've painted a tributary mural of the Statue of Liberty on the sunny, yellow walls.

You'll still hear the old tongue spoken here, where Ukrainian sausages are the pride of the meat case, sharing space with other Old World favorites such as leberkaase, blutwurst, and shinkenspeck, along with house-made picnic brats. Caraway rye and sweet kolachi star among the baked goods that hark back to a Slavic kitchen.

And for the hordes who would rather not fuss with cooking, the cafeteria line in an adjacent room provides hearty homesick cures like borscht, goulash soup, sauerkraut with ham, red cabbage, and an array of dumplings.

ing of tables draw the arts and media statement-makers of the cities as well as foodies of all stripes. It's become a destination.

Warmly opinionated waitresses are free with advice on the appealing menu. They'll tell you that the don't-miss dish is the pot roast, updated from Mom's version. Jim serves it with garlic mashed potatoes, roasted vegetables, and a horseradish-sour cream sauce. His hefty pork shanks come with squash puree and a warm balsamic vinaigrette. Vegetarians go for his ravioli, often stuffed with mushrooms, atop a sherry-carrot puree, or the perennially popular mac and cheese, updated with Italian taleggio cheese, mushrooms, and truffle oil. See what I mean?

The Modern's standout breakfast items include pampered eggs, such as a scramble showcasing cream cheese, bacon, and more mushrooms. The kitchen's morning hash features a rerun of that dandy pot roast, shredded and tossed with potatoes, eggs, and other good eats.

Desserts include a cinnamon crème brûlée (called "custard" in the good old days), an apple crisp served warm with vanilla ice cream, and a flourless chocolate torte. There's nothing 40s about Jim's wine list. It's laced with interesting labels at prices Nordeasterners can swallow. And on weekly wine nights, every bottles sells for half the regular price.

NYE'S POLONAISE ROOM

112 East Hennepin Avenue, Minneapolis
(612) 379-2021 • nyespolonaise.com
$$; M

NYE'S IS MORE THAN a place to eat and drink, it's an institution. Polish immigrant Al Nye launched his supper club in 1949, back when Northeast Minneapolis was still Nordeast, a blue-collar, working-class neighborhood of first- and second-generation settlers from the Old Country who were proud of their Old-World ties.

Not much has changed since then, and that's what makes the Polonaise Room worth a visit. From the red neon grand piano logo to Lil Snider, the septuagenarian with a blond bouffant who plays oldies to the exuberant admiration of her sing-along fans clustered around her piano, the ambience hasn't altered a whit. Not the deep, curvy, gold-spangled booths. Not the red velvet wallpaper and Naugahyde to match. Not the sparkly chandeliers. Not the veteran servers like Gina, the hostess for over 25 years, nor silver-haired server Fran, who's hoisted those overflowing trays for 18 seasons. (When asked for the wine list, she'll offer this guidance: "You don't want wine here, honey.") And certainly not the menu.

The food carries a hearty Polish accent, as in sauerkraut with short ribs and maybe the best (unquestionably the heftiest) liver and onions in town. Hunters' stew (a.k.a. bigos, the Polish national dish) comes loaded with lots of tender beef and slow-cooked Polish sausage mingling with sauerkraut, cabbage, mushrooms, onions, tomato, and garlic, all served in a traditional silver pot and ladled over rice. Celebration of the homeland's kitchen continues with ham steak, pork hocks, kielbasa sausage, cabbage rolls, and plenty of other plates that defy a dainty diet. All include choice of soup or salad, a hearty relish tray, boiled potatoes, and a warm loaf of Polish rye. Nye's pierogi assortment proves just as winning; it's a platter of those flaky pastries filled with sauerkraut, potato, and prunes, served with a generous side of sour cream.

But the specialty—ask Fran—is Nye's cut of prime rib: 32 ounces of blush-pink beef, along with all the fixings of a supper club from yesteryear. Daily specials range from meatloaf and mashed potatoes to roast pork loin with homemade dressing. Oh well, once the band strikes up, you can polka all those calories away.

Today, thanks to its proximity to the University of Minnesota campus, Nye's has been rediscovered by a student population in search of kitsch, who crowd around Lil like their parents did. Yet the place has never really gone out of fashion, with scads of near-fanatic regulars of the older generation, twisting and twirling to the polka band, who can't get enough of the nostalgia quotient—food, drinks, ambience, and music—which is far more than the sum of its parts.

ODDFELLOWS

401 East Hennepin Avenue, Minneapolis
(612) 378-3179 • oddfellowsrestaurant.com
$$

ODDFELLOWS IS THE KIND of cosmopolitan café that lets people dream they're in a secret haunt in the heart of SoHo, far from Ea Henn—East Hennepin—in the Minneapple. Yet the understated chic of the intimate dining room could soothe a New Yorker in search of class.

The brick façade on the newly happening East Hennepin corridor is prelude to a vintage ceiling of stamped tin, with walls in tones as warm as honey, hung with splashes of original art. Marble-topped tables, thoughtfully spaced to induce quiet conversation, circle the blond bar in the rear, serving cutting-edge couples, gay and straight, who've adopted the comfy setting as their club. But membership is wide open, as the friendly servers indicate.

They know their way around the dreamy wine list, too. It's loaded with its share of odd fellows worth investigating, such as the quirky Rough and Ready label, which lives up to its name.

Back in the kitchen, they're a bunch of experimenters, always on to the next odd combination of quality ingredients, creating dishes that cause diners to gasp, "How do they do that?" and also, upon occasion, "Why?" A wild mushroom ragout with black lentils laced with balsamic vinegar is one of the best things ever to cross a palate, and the "martini" of salmon tartare spiked with tequila and a jolt of guajillo peppers is good enough to bring grown men to tears. A wasabi-painted ahi tuna, paired with a tamari beurre blanc, plays the yin-yang of biting horseradish against the soothing, nutty sauce—another hit. Even the falafel makes one forget those dreary patties of the past. These almost float to the table, buoyed by cilantro and chipotles, set off with a side of cool, crisp cucumber relish and a splash of tahini laced with honey. (And for those who like to take it nice and easy, Oddfellows offers beef with mashed potatoes.)

In the wrong hands, chicken can be dry as Styrofoam. Not here. Given a rub of spices, the breast is juicy and flavorful. But a maple mole verde sauce? Lay caution aside and trust your server's urging, and one is very likely to discover that the dish is right on the money. Odd fellows again, but in the right saucepan, opposites attract.

Chef Matthew Williams and general manager Paul Kost have a winner on their hands, and it's fun to serve as judge and jury when they see how far they can push the envelope. Kost also manages the adjoining Boom! nightclub, whose pulsing beat and dusky lighting seem distant, thanks to an entryway that sends diners to the left for peace and quiet and dancers to the right to spin the night away.

POP!

2859 NE Johnson Street, Minneapolis
(612) 788-0455 • poprestaurant.com
$–$$; F

POP!, THE SWEET LITTLE restaurant that recently added fizz to the underserved Northeast stretch of the city, deserves those eye-catching capital letters and exclamation point—possibly chosen in homage to the Warhol-inspired pop art on the warm, sunny walls.

The tiny corner café began life way back when as a drugstore with a soda fountain, then morphed into a longstanding pizzeria before the new owner, in a euphoria of ambition and elbow grease, extensively remodeled the place. Today its walls shimmer with bold tones of khaki, tangerine, and marine blue. Chair seats adopt the same vibrant hues, showcased against lots of blond wood lighting up the tabletops and shiny floors. Silvery duct pipes hover just below the pressed-tin ceiling, also hung with schoolhouse globes of light. The café's two narrow rooms share energy through a cutaway niche. A small kitchen, partly in view, speaks to the freshness of the food.

POP!'s flavors are as bright as the surroundings. Taking inspiration from warm and sunny parts of the Americas, starters lead off with a satisfying chicken posole soup warmed with a hint of chiles and an equally hearty black bean rendition. Jerk chicken wings graduate from mere bar food, thanks to a dipping sauce of cilantro mango foam. Picadillo empanadas, served with a lively chimichurri sauce, compete with a trio of seviches for your favor.

Salads globetrot to Cuba and Thailand, then boomerang straight back to Nordeast with a traditional wedge of iceberg glossed with thousand-island dressing. It's the same story with entrées: Test an adventurous palate with shrimp on Israeli couscous, paired with chorizo and an olive relish; a Mexican ropa vieja of shredded beef stewed in tomato sauce; or matambre, grilled steak with garbanzo beans, blue cheese, and chimichurri. Or hike the straight-and-narrow with—yes—Swedish meatballs. They're served with mashed potatoes and lingonberries, the true Scando way. And they're good.

AL'S BREAKFAST

413 14th Avenue SE • Minneapolis • (612) 331-9991

Al's is a University of Minnesota campus institution. In fact, it may be illegal to graduate if you haven't eaten here. Even after 50-plus years of slinging eggs and hash browns, the eponymous Dinkytown diner still packs the stools, all 14 of them. The sidewalk, too, is clogged with wannabes as alums return to the scene of many a cheap and filling early-morning campus feed. The sass delivered with your java is as legendary as the tiny diner's nondécor, which consists of grease spots amid photos and postcards from faraway fans who'd rather be here. Don't be unnerved by the hordes looming over your counter stool as you reach for the salt; they'll get their share of lip from the help behind the counter soon enough.

But then, so's the salmon stuffed with shiitakes, wrapped in nori (seaweed) and wontons and plated with a coconut curry sauce. And the straight-arrow pastas are not to be overlooked, either.

No matter what, dessert is a must. POP!'s pastry chef comes with a diploma from the Culinary Institute of America, enabling her to manage with utmost finesse such creations as crepes filled with dulce de leche and candied hazelnuts; a chocolate tres leches with bananas and plantain chips; and a homey tapioca pudding gone Caribbean with coconut, roasted pineapple, and passion fruit. There's chocolate pecan pie with coffee con leche sauce and a molten chocolate cake, worth the eight minutes' wait, if you can stand it, served upon a roasted banana pudding and topped with coconut-chocolate sauce.

Wine, beer, and soft drinks are as reasonable as the food prices, all delivered by friendly, chatty servers who probably live a block away.

RESTAURANT ALMA

528 University Avenue SE, Minneapolis
(612) 379-4909 • restaurantalma.com
$$; P; O

ALMA MEANS "NOURISHING" and "cherishing," a fitting title for this sweetheart of a restaurant, which is all about real food. Alma nourishes its guests—oh, does it ever!—and cherishes its artisanal purveyors. In fact, its menu notes its commitment to "sustainable agriculture, local farms and producers, and conservation efforts."

Even the design of the brick storefront speaks to these beliefs. A row of slender birch trees against the wall of what was once a small meat market offers living testimony, as do vases thick with sunflowers among the banquettes and tables, some with a view of the hard-working kitchen. (There's also mezzanine seating for larger parties.)

Young chef/co-owner Alex Roberts lists the East Coast on his resume, but he's clearly fallen in love with the heartlands, as evidenced by his short, frequently changing and appealing menu. Waitresses, more like moms than hired servers, have diners' best interests at heart; they'll tell folks what not to miss, or which wine, from the equally engaging and unusual list, pairs well with a dish. They'll praise starters like the kitchen's now-legendary bruschetta, which never leaves the menu; it's topped with chicken liver pâté, apricots, bacon, and a sage-port wine jus. Or consider the thin-crust grilled pizza, topped with roasted butternut squash, herbed mascarpone, pecorino and Romano cheeses, and duck confit. Ahi tuna appears quickly seared, then served with shaved fennel,

WILDE ROAST

518 East Hennepin Avenue • Minneapolis • (612) 331-4544

Wilde Roast, named in honor of the iconoclastic Irish writer, Oscar, is a wild card on the stretch of Hennepin Avenue where blue-collar Nordeast meets the hipsters of southeast—a blending and bonding of eclectic demographics in a hybrid (just like Oscar) site that's part coffeehouse, part wine bar, and part café. They come together in a Victorian setting that centers on a working fireplace, comfy, overstuffed chairs, lots of mahogany accents, and a row of tables as closely packed as the proverbial sardines. Order and pay at the counter for tableside delivery of coffee, wine, and house-made eats beginning with breakfast standbys like frittatas, sour cream coffee cake, and French toast enriched (like it needs it!) with peaches, dark cherries, and cinnamon. The lunch-to-late-night menu features quesadillas, deli sandwiches, designer pizzas, and giant salads as well as house-made desserts as decadent as the hangout's namesake. Stick around for the readings, too.

snappy Chinese mustard, and an aromatic ginger dressing, or perhaps as a tartare with lemon confit, tarragon, more fennel, and root vegetable chips. The tomato bread soup is another hit.

As main courses, which Alex garnishes with loads of TLC, chicken works, because it's of the tasty, free-range tribe, served with soft polenta, sautéed greens, chorizo sausage, and caper berries. The duck confit reappears, along with a meaty breast, accompanied by savoy cabbage, salsify, and a rosemary-apple puree. The kitchen does especially well with seafood, as proven by pan-roasted diver scallops upon risotto laced with shreds of peeky toe crab, along with fennel and broccoli in a subtle saffron sauce. On another day, those same scallops will partner with wild pink shrimp, zucchini, and tomatoes in a truf-fled herb broth. In spring, look for roast lamb and grilled lamb sausage rest-ing on polenta, along with wine-braised onions, chard, and golden raisins.

Vegetarians come away satisfied after feasting on a celery root and potato gratin, sided with fresh vegetables and chestnuts in black truffle sauce, or masa corn crepes stuffed with ricotta and braised greens, smoked portobellos, and lentils, all accented by a suave poblano cream.

Fair warning about desserts: They succeed. And they're not your run-of-the-pastry cart staples. Instead, try the star anise and black cardamom custard tart served with a syrah-poached pear and prunes steeped in bourbon-vanilla tea. Or buttermilk panna cotta with passion fruit jelly. A plate of artisanal cheeses—a menu rarity in local restaurants— is another grand option, with dessert wines by the glass for pairing.

Diners stream in from the nearby university campus, so one finds profs mingling with politicos, arts funders, and just plain Joes and Janes who savor the care Alma takes in the kitchen and on the dining floor.

THE SAMPLE ROOM

2124 NE Marshall Street, Minneapolis
(612) 789-0333
$–$$

THE SAMPLE ROOM takes its name from its history. The handsome brick two-story building close by the Mississippi River in northeast Minneapolis was built in 1893 as the Thies Hotel and Sample Room. It's where the traveling salesmen of the day headed to spread out their wares, such as sample bolts of cloth, for customers, and then take a room for the night upstairs and repair to the saloon at the corner.

But the deeds go back even further. In 1849, Henry Sibley and his wife, Sarah, bought the lot from the U.S. government. In between these bookends, it passed through the hands of John Orth, whose Orth Brewery was the predecessor of the Grain Belt Company, and to Gottfried Gluek, who launched Gluek Brewery in 1857.

Today it's a saloon again, in the old-fashioned, neighborhood-gathering sense, and also a culinary sample room. Almost every dish from the ambitious kitchen is offered in sample-portion sizes—call it the Midwest version of tapas if you will. And they're designed for nibbling and sharing as folks once again congregate here among the dark woooden tables and booths that don't stray far from the old-time bar.

These tastes, on the left side of the menu, are subdivided by category, priced per plate or at a value for a choice of any four. Among cheeses, select from dry-aged Sonoma jack, baked Stickney Hill goat cheese drizzled with oven-dried tomatoes and basil oil, or warm camembert with caramelized onions, all the way to Not Your Mom's Mac & Cheese. Then on to the meats, which segue from grilled homemade poultry sausage, braised pork ribs with whiskey-tomato sauce, or homemade country pâté to warm baked ham or chilled turkey breast—traditional Minnesota dishes with an eye to quality. Seafood snacks include mussels Provençal, crab cakes with red pepper sour cream, and seared rare tuna with wasabi aioli and house-made gravlax. Vegetarians are fortunate in their choices, too, with green beans with sesame and tamari, roasted fennel and red potato salad, and a wild mushroom pâté among the standouts.

Soups and meal-sized salads lead the right-hand list, followed by sandwich classics—from burgers to grilled cheese—as well as contemporary spins on walleye or portobello mushrooms on a bun. Entrées, for the hungry eater or the guy who just won't share, include traditional saloon favorites such as roasted turkey, braised pork ribs, meatloaf, and baked walleye. But truth to tell, they're probably just for show. Most fans find the same appealing flavors among the sample plates.

Desserts are predictable, and huge—carrot cake, chocolate layer cake—plus a pair of crème brûlées in changing flavors.

The sample concept continues to the beverages list, where wine and Scotch by flights add to the sense of experimentation. Of course, it wouldn't be a saloon without beer, and the Sample Room complies.

Count on a crack waitstaff for advice if the menu appears overwhelming; they eat here, and they know what's really good.

UDUPI

4920 Central Avenue NE, Minneapolis
(763) 574-1113 • www.udupicafemn.com
$; P; F

DON'T JUDGE A BOOK by its cover, they say, and don't judge an Indian restaurant by its setting. The look may be Country Kitchen—unassuming white façade, knotty pine, brick veneer—but the food comes from the traditional country kitchens of Southern India and their vegetarian heritage. And it's some of the very best of its kind—make that, any kind—in the Midwest, right here on the fringe of Northeast Minneapolis. A most mannerly team of gentlemen have put the enterprise together; in their crisp white shirts, black vests, and ties, their dress is as professional as their solicitous deportment.

Overseeing the expanse of tables, laid with white cloths and sprigs of silk flowers, are poster portraits of Hindu deities, framed by twinkling lights. They smile down on an audience just as eclectic as the décor—many native Indians, seeking authentic flavors of their homeland, mixed with college students, retirees on a budget, and suited-up professionals, alongside truckers and fellows in the building trades who are particular aficionados of the tasty noontime buffet.

For first-timers, or the terminally undecided, a trio of composed Thali dinners provides a sampling of the kitchen's fortes. Or venture down the list of appetizers, all served with a lively chutney (tamarind, tomato, and coconut among the choices) and a lightly spicy sambar soup. Iddly—steamed rice and lentil patties—serve both as palate-cleansers and as sponges for the litany of delicious sauces.

Dosai, the light crepes also fashioned from rice and lentils, come in a myriad of flavors; they can be topped with onions or hot chutney, filled with chilies and potatoes, and layered with vegetables. Pullaus, the region's rice specialties, range from a vegetable biryani to tamarind rice melded with hot-and-sour sauce and a crunch of peanuts. Uthappam pancakes are treated to another rainbow of seasonings, with onions, peas, tomatoes, and chiles. And almost a meal in themselves are the Indian breads—deep-fried whole-wheat poori, paratha stuffed with spiced potatoes, and many more.

And we haven't even spoken of the currries yet. Served with tart yogurt and sweet-spicy pickles, they range from a mix of cauliflower and potatoes to eggplant pureed with onions and tomatoes, on to spinach laced with homemade cheese or lentils brightened with mustard and cumin, plus a dozen more. Vegan options are clearly marked.

The rice pudding is beyond your grandma's—here, it's a royal dessert. Just as traditional and tasty is the basmalai, a sweet sweet indeed, fashioned from homemade cottage cheese flavored with rose water; the deep-fried version laced in a light syrup; a specialty composed of vermicelli cooked with milk and honey; or crunchy halvah.

Wine (very basic) and Indian beers are available, as is lassi, the favorite Indian yogurt drink, served either sweet or salted. Or succumb to a fresh mango shake or an invigorating lemon drink composed of freshly squeezed fruit, sugar, and soda water. Indian-spiced tea makes for easy sipping, too.

CHAPTER THREE

Uptown and Nicollet Areas
Minneapolis

AURIGA

1930 Hennepin Avenue South, Minneapolis
(612) 871-0777 • aurigarestaurant.com
$$$; O; P

AURIGA IS THE NAME of a heavenly constellation—quite fitting for this shining star in Uptown's diadem of restaurants. Reborn with a new lease on dining life from the days of what old-timers may recall as Becky's Cafeteria, in its current incarnation this cheery spot fast became a favorite of nearby Kenwood residents and arts aficionados seeking a tasteful bite en route to the Walker Art Center.

The sunny yellow exterior is prelude to a series of rooms garbed in warm, earthy hues. One captures the passing crowd on Hennepin Avenue through a veil that shelters diners from sidewalk voyeurs, while the other, slightly more spacious and private, simply scans the parking lot—itself a blessing in this crowded neighborhood. (It's also the cityscape site of a small, leafy dining patio drafted into use in summer.) A small bar, dressed in the blue of a midnight sky, does double duty as a foyer. Here regulars gather to sip wine by the glass and, if time allows, enjoy the full menu from the restaurant's inventive kitchen.

It's headed by executive chef Doug Flicker—that's Doug is his trademark, beat-up stevedore's knit cap—a bright luminary on the city's dining scene. When reopening in spring, 2005 after a lengthy and ambitious remodeling project, he and his team introduced a new and vastly more ambitions menu, too. No longer primarily a pleasant pizza/pasta café with starters and entrees "just in case," the gentrified list (that could float in Manhattan) now leads off with *amuses*—tiny pre-app bites such as a truffled dwarf white peach with pecorino and arugula or smoked salmon ravioli with whipped ricotta and white truffle sea salt.

Larger starters include a poached duck egg partnered with haricots verts, arbequino olives and gazpacho sauce, and preserved local foie gras sent out in three discrete bites, paired first with Serrano ham, then quince pasta and finally, fried hazelnuts. Three pizzas from the former menu made the cut, leading with a signature topping of smoked pheasant, Swiss chard, asparagus and pecorino. The kitchen's famed Caesar salad remains, thank your lucky stars, joined this round by a plate of butter lettuce tossed with shaved parmesan and pancetta.

Wisely, the entrée selection is still kept short and sweet: chicken with artichoke ravioli and French apple sausages; Fischer Farms pork in a chestnut and asparagus ragout; pheasant paired with dates, gnocchi and kale; and tuna rubbed with anchovy-garlic paste, then topped with porcini mushrooms.

Desserts calm down a little, for folks, not matter how soigné, still want their chocolate cake (here, with hazelnut mascarpone mousse) and cheesecake (a slice of white chocolate-licorice filling on a pistachio crust), leaders on a list abetted by a coconut caramel cream and slice of artisanal cheese.

Weeknights, the "new" Auriga provides five-, seven- and nine-course degustation menus as well. And the wine list of well-suited labels, strong in Spanish and Italian appellations, is offered at fair value. Savvy and attentive servers get arts patrons in and out in a jiffy, yet let business moguls and romantic assignations linger in the shadows to order another cappuccino as cool jazz drifts from the speakers into the night.

BAR ABILENE

1300 Lagoon Avenue, Minneapolis
(612) 825-2525 • barabilene.com
$$; O; P

BAR ABILENE is the rowdy kid managed by the same restaurant family that sired Goodfellow's, where fine dining reigns, and Tejas, offering well-bred Southwestern cuisine to those in the suburbs. Spunky Bar Abilene fits its Uptown mold—high energy, informal, and uncomplicated, providing a vibrant scene for singles and just a whole lot of fun.

That's not enough to make the cut, however. It's run by pros who train (and train and train) its ranch hands how to serve. And that starts with smiles as big as Texas.

This Uptown riff on a Texas saloon is done with tongue-in-cheek, sashaying from longhorn skulls and coiled lariats on the adobe-tinted walls to miniature covered wagons trailing along the tops of room dividers. Pots of cactus bristle in the corners, and black-and-white TVs play nostalgic Westerns (sans sound, so you can hear what your tablemates are saying).

In summer the sidewalk tables make for good people-watching over a basket of chips and a longneck as crowds surge past to the nearby art cinema. Gazing out of floor-to-ceiling windows at a wintry Sunday brunch is almost as good as an art flick, too.

It's a full sensory experience, all right, but the bottom line is all about the food. And those who cannot tell a poblano from a chipotle need not fear. The menu segues from Tex-Mex comfort fare (burritos, fajitas, enchiladas) to all-American hits, including burgers, Caesar salad, and calamari. But in the fine

SEBASTIAN JOE'S

1007 Franklin Avenue West • Minneapolis • (612) 870-0065
4321 Upton Avenue South • Minneapolis • (612) 926-7916

This company taught the Twin Cities all it knows about homemade gourmet ice cream. The Uptown shop has been scooping since the late 80s, later backed up by a second location in Linden Hills. The ice cream empire, which now serves many a local restaurant as well as hordes of heck-with-dieting cone-lickers, was the brainchild of three brothers, Tim, Todd, and Mike Pellizzer. They named their venture in honor of their Italian grandfather, who knows all there is to know about gelato.

He'd probably relish the zillion rotating varieties, made the classic, Old-Country way—intense in flavor and easy to love. But the boys have marched out New-World inventions, too, segueing from banana yogurt and grapefruit-campari sorbet to Pavarotti, the hands-down bestseller, melding caramel, banana, and chocolate chips into one sinful scoop.

The popular neighborhood hangout also features a complete menu of coffee drinks to savor while perusing newspapers on a stick and stacks of journals.

print, it's clear that the kitchen has raised the table stakes for originality. The calamari come laced with wasabi and a smoked tomato aioli. The burger's topped with house-made guacamole, and the salad with cayenne croutons.

Yet it's the Southwestern fare that stands out, including starters like a chipotle barbecued-shrimp taco with jicama relish and cilantro sour cream or a roasted chicken and poblano pesto quesadilla with organic tomato salsa. Bar Abilene's signature guacamole is prepared tableside, another swell prelude to entrées that include oven-roasted chicken with papaya chutney, Southwestern rice and black beans, or a ranch-cut beef tenderloin with tamarind steak sauce, roasted-garlic whipped potatoes, and cayenne onion rings.

Desserts, as huge as J.R.'s ranch, include a chocolate ancho diablo cake that carries a bit of a fiery punch and a moist, rich coconut tres leches cake served with pineapple soaked in rum and a cactus pear sauce.

The beer list is long and strong, as is the catalog of margaritas, but where Bar Abilene takes the lead is in its signature collection of tequilas, many aged for decades. Both connoisseurs and experts-in-the-making may extend their pleasure, and their education, by ordering tasting samplers.

The saying in Abilene, Texas is, "Y'all come back." It works here, too.

BLACK FOREST INN

1 East 26th Street, Minneapolis
(612) 872-0812 • blackforestinnmpls.com
$–$$; O

THE BLACK FOREST INN is more than a German restaurant (and the best in the metro at that). It's been a cultural—make that, a countercultural—icon, serving heaping bowls of goulash and steins of beer that test a weight lifter's capabilities to art students and poets-in-the-making since it threw open its Bavarian shutters 40 years ago. Back then, the young idealists gathered to quote Zen or to practice their college German with the owner, Erich Christ, a butcher from the Old Country. In fact, that's how Erich met JoAnne, who became his wife and partner.

The murals of pine-fringed Bavarian lakes and castles were done, I'll wager, to pay an artist's bar tab. They accent the dark wood interior with well-worn plank flooring and a colony of tables overlaid with cloths of red on green. It's the land of the Student Prince, from beveled glass to stained-glass artworks, lots of shields and coats of arms, and, of course, and the mandatory stag's head gazing at a painted ceiling, courtesy of a budding Rubens.

To assure that all these Teutonic emblems of gemütlichkeit aren't taken all too seriously, there's also the cheeky life-sized photomural, now a local legend, of the ladies of the DAR. There's also a patio, where checked tablecloths appear amid the arboreal setting as soon as the ice breaks on the Mississippi. It's here the students (and the parents and professors of students) love to gather under the stars.

Erich, the former butcher, still cuts his meat into portions judged mammoth, even by Minnesota standards. Bulk it up on dishes like his famous handmade bratwurst or giant meatballs (konigsberger klops) as big as grapefruit. The pork shank puts even those to shame, as does the thick-sliced, smoky rippchen (pork chop). And yes, they come with all the German add-ons heaped upon your plate.

From sauerbraten to rouladen, schnitzel to spaetzle, it's food from the original Black Forest, a message further underscored by German potato salad in the traditional bacon-vinegar dressing, sauerkraut (even—gasp!—sauerkraut balls, which go down better after a pilsner or two), and a hearty wurst salad. It wouldn't be the Black Forest without the region's signature Black Forest cherry torte, a four-layer indulgence made even wickeder by thick slatherings of buttercream. Sacher torte, the flourless cake born in Vienna, is another classic from the kitchen, as is the flaky apple strudel and cheesecakes, German-style, all lovingly made by the inn's own baking staff. The adjoining Strudel & Nudel deli offers all these, and more, on a take-home basis so folks can enjoy their own dinner parties.

BRYANT LAKE BOWL

810 West Lake Street, Minneapolis
(612) 825-3737 • bryantlakebowl.com
$; M

NO ONE HAS EVER accused proprietor Kim Bartman of lacking imagination. When she chose a blue-collar bowling alley ten years ago as the site of her café, folks went, "Huh?"

She kept the bowling alley as an active operation, turned the bar space fronting it into a funky café, and added an avant-garde mini-theater to the side. Now there's something for everyone, right?

Well, almost. The Bud-drinking guys in the former leagues may not be her best customers since they've discovered the hip Gen Xers drinking espresso and Veuve Cliquot as they roll their strikes and spares, but the rest of Uptown's singular singles, gay and straight, have lined up to fill their (bowling) shoes.

Shrewdly, Kim retained the vintage working-class décor: well-trod flooring of fading black and red squares, retro starlight ceiling fixtures, the worn wooden bar that's absorbed its share of war stories, and an array of gleaming trophies lined above it. She's added a snazzy, 40s-style bowling mural up there, too.

Beer, sure: It wouldn't be a bowling alley without it. But these days the lineup features microbrews and imports, many on draught. The wine list is just as selective (including that Veuve Cliquot to celebrate a winning score), and the cappuccino machine stays more than busy.

The music fits the eclectic crowd, too—anything from Frankie to hip-hop, but played softly enough to hear the pins fall in the rear and to support the intense, soul-searching conversations that often occur here.

THE TIN FISH

Lake Calhoun • 3000 East Calhoun Parkway • Minneapolis
(612) 370-4883 • seasonal only

Order up: Cup of chowder, fish and chips, and a kayak. It's possible—
and popular—at the new Tin Fish, which opened in summer 2004 in
Lake Calhoun's inviting but hitherto-unappreciated pavilion. Chosen
by the city to make a go of a failing concession stand, the new outfit
offers cones and cold drinks but a whole lot more, and at most
attractive prices.

Fish tacos feature a selection of six varieties of seafood. Grilled or
combo platters include fish and chips, natch (and make that salmon,
halibut, cod, walleye, or a mixed plate), as well as shrimp, scallops,
oysters, calamari, and fillets, served with slaw and tartar sauce.
They're also proud to have resurrected the legendary Rainbow Café
burger, a formula deeded to them as relatives of the former historic
restaurant's owners.

Trot your tray to one of the outdoor tables—choose sun or the shade of
the pavilion—for a ringside view of the lake while you're licking hot
sauce from your fingers. Kids' menu, too. Oh, and kayak/canoe rentals.

After ten years in business, the menu has changed very little. It's fresh
and fun. Appetizer snacks include homemade chili, quesadillas, and the
Bryant Lake Bowl plate, laden with smoked trout, roasted garlic, dill havarti
cheese, and grilled baguettes. Sandwiches run from the standard—Reubens
and Rachels and a tuna melt—to a Philly built of shaved organic bison and
a California burger that takes on a local character with grass-fed beef from
Minnesota Moonstone Farms.

The entrée list, while short, does not succumb to sameness, either. Bowlers
and poets may sup on grilled tuna served on ginger-infused spinach with
roasted garlic mashed potatoes and hoisin sauce, and at half the price a fancy
restaurant would charge. Among the many vegetarian options are the spinach,
feta, and artichoke pasta, a bowl of pad Thai, or a husky bean burrito.

The good news is, Bryant Lake Bowl serves breakfast like you wouldn't believe. And the new gets even better: It's served till 3 p.m. Egg scrambles and omelets lead the list, with loads of options. Or try the homemade granola, lush with nuts and craisins, or the French toast formed of crusty baguettes. Your waitress—the one in jeans with the spiky hair—is happy to accommodate.

CAFÉ BARBETTE

1600 West Lake Street, Minneapolis
(612) 827-5710 • barbette.com
$–$$; O

BARBETTE IS YOUR ARCHETYPAL alternative urban hangout, well beloved by Uptown's artsy singles as a meeting place and equally populated by the couples of Kenwood who habitually congregate here. Transplant Barbette to SoHo and it wouldn't be out of place.

Although it began life as a coffeehouse, the enterprise soon morphed into a complete, three-meal café. The singular setting remains intact: terrazzo flooring below heavy ceiling beams slicked with blue, from which faux cut-glass lanterns dangle. A theatrical burgundy curtain acts as an entry, leading to a scattering of tables against the leatherette banquettes and a curvy golden counter for seating, diner-style, at the bar. The back wall serves as palette for a series of changing art displays by local painters. And the picture windows framing the passing parade on Lake Street provide Uptown's version of performance art.

Dinner may be as light or elaborate as a diner chooses. Those in the soup-and-salad mode can find satisfaction with a bowl of French onion loaded with cheese and a classic Caesar salad. Or make a meal of a salade Niçoise as done in France, with tuna that doesn't come from a can, along with baby green beans, purple potatoes, and a quail egg—well, maybe that's a regional addition. So is the plate of smoked Wisconsin trout, served with fingerling potatoes on frisee daubed with crème fraiche and chive oil.

Or begin with oysters, fried or on the half-shell, to pave the way for a Croque Monsieur (or Madame), one of the few authentic renditions of the grilled French sandwich in town.

Leading the list of hearty entrées, the wild mushroom risotto, perfumed with truffle oil, makes classy comfort food. Barbette is equally renowned for the kitchen's way with steak frites. And because the chef pays homage to local artisanal providers, the roast chicken really tastes like chicken ought to. So do the flown-in-fresh fish selections, which vary daily. And there's always a vegetarian offering.

Other Parisian bistro fare includes crepes with choice of filling, an espresso chocolate fondue for two, and a textbook-perfect crème caramel. Count on Barbette for wine finds, too—well-selected labels from all over the globe at excellent value.

Barbette also welcomes guests for breakfast—often taken on the sidewalk tables in the heat of summer. Oatmeal, the hearty, old-fashioned kind, heads the selections, which include homemade granola, fruit salad, quiche of the day, and breakfast pastries. And, thanks to the original coffeehouse days, count on a darned good brew.

Servers, clad as informally as those who jog in here, are caregivers, for sure. They're warmly trained by proprietor Kim Bartman, who also owns the Bryant Lake Bowl.

CAMPIELLO

1320 West Lake Street, Minneapolis
(612) 825-2222

6411 City West Parkway, Eden Prairie
(952) 941-6868 • damico.com
$$; P; O

CAMPIELLO IS THE BREEZY Tuscan cousin of the D'Amico brothers' urban, Milan-inspired D'Amico Cucina. But there's no need to wait for a special occasion to drop in at this pair of casual trattorias to experience the same commitment to quality ingredients and careful preparations as the swank original. Here the scene imparts a movie-set version of a venerable Italian piazza, propped with a sea of densely packed tables clad in butcher paper and surrounded by walls warmed in caffe latte tones. There's also a small side room, straight from a Fellini film—a romantic nook dressed in graceful chandeliers and cushy drapes, away from the clamor, where it's easier to carry on a conversation. In the summertime, a small patio off the parking lot draws alfresco diners, too.

And they come in all flavors—three-generation family groups, twosomes, foursomes, girls' night out—to mix and mingle as they would in Italy, spurred by the high-energy surroundings designed as a tip of the hat to the dining demands of this gimme-entertainment-with-my-dinner crowd. To do so, an open kitchen captures the sous chefs in their dash from rotisserie to woodburning oven: you see the sizzle as well as the steak. And in the rear, a small bar serves as prelude/postlude to a meal. Its trendy martini list is almost as lengthy as the menu itself.

This dining list takes its cue from a true Italian menu, beginning with appetizers such as bruschetta strewn with tomatoes, basil, capers, and garlic, on to fried baby artichokes to spritz with lemon, or calamari to swipe through a suave aioli. Delicate, thin-crusted pizzas are another starter option, clad in classic toppings and finished in that oak-fired oven.

Toasted semolina croutons set Campiello's Caesar salad apart, while the Caprese rendition, built of fresh tomatoes, house-made mozzarella, and snippets of basil, rivals many a plate in Rome. A half-dozen pastas follow, available in starter or entrée portions; they salute the kitchen's proven favorites, such as ravioli filled with butternut squash and sent out with a sage brown butter; penne with chicken from the spit joined by herbs and artichokes; or a hearty ragu, sometimes based on boar, to top the pliant noodles.

Hearty cuts of pork and beef come grilled or roasted in true Tuscan style, to join house specialties like balsamic-glazed short ribs, a lamb shank paired the Old Country way with risotto Milanese, or seafood highlighted by a sea bass served with stewed baby artichokes and potato puree—a dish to dream about.

Desserts toe the line, beginning with a velvety panna cotta and warm chocolate truffle cake and ending with ice cream or sorbetti with a bonus of biscotti on the side. The Uptown location, across the street from the Lagoon Theater, makes dinner and a movie more than mundane.

CHINO LATINO

2919 Hennepin Avenue South, Minneapolis
(612) 824-PUPU • chinolatino.com
$$; valet parking

IN A SWAGGER OF HIPNESS and ultracool, there's not even a name on the front of this establishment. Like the "in" clientele of a fancy New York club, you just have to know. But here in egalitarian Minnesota, everybody does. (The sassy billboards around town don't hurt.) It's the storefront blazing with undulating gold glitter.

Inside, to continue the speakeasy mode, diner wannabes must make their way down a narrow corridor before the host stand comes in sight.

It's there the sizzle begins. Chino Latino is a leader in the "eat-ertainment" concept, transformed into a shimmering palace of eye candy that ricochets from

PHO 79

2529 Nicollet Avenue South • Minneapolis • (612) 871-4602

Pho (pronounced "fuh") is the national dish of Vietnam—a warm and hearty beef soup that, folklore has it, will cure whatever ails you, from a hangover to a broken heart. It's built upon a steamy broth laced with slender rice noodles, fresh bean sprouts, basil, lime, and a subtle hit of hot peppers. And pho is what Pho 79 is all about. The special 79 version of this comfort food marries rare, lean beef, well-done flank, fat brisket, soft tendons, tripe, and meatballs with the basic ingredients. The tiny outfit also offers diners other variations on the theme, as well as a few more Vietnamese staples, but why stray? Folks come here for pho.

the glowing, shades-of-Hades bar to the back wall shimmering with ruby votive candles; the make-an-entrance staircase descending to the lower level; and the satay counter, which produces tidbits of grilled meat on skewers to accompany those outrageous umbrella drinks. Cast an eye to the lower level in the atrium with its clever cocoon booths for six or eight and the long communal table for the lively and diverse medley of singles who gravitate here, winking over the non-PC bathrooms and naughty fortune cookies. Those over 30 may strain to make themselves heard in the din.

Created by chef Michael Larson, who also oversees Chino's elder cousin, Figlio, across the street, the menu salutes "street food from the hot zones"—an homage to Asia, Latin America, and the South Pacific. He's foregone the tempting route of fusion in favor of a mosaic of flavors more or less true to their roots. Portions are colossal (you order jerk chicken and you get the whole bird) and meant for sharing.

Appetizers with a global cast include Chinese barbecued ribs, chicken enchiladas, Cuban black bean soup, Saigon spring rolls, and the ultimate: the Big Kahuna pupu platter (remember those?).

Continue the sharing with even bigger entrée platters, such as the powerhouse tequila chipotle shrimp, justly marked with a firecracker to indicate its potency, or Mekong mahimahi lettuce wraps, Philippine paella, Montego Bay jerk chicken served with black beans, rice, and plantains, and a gaucho-sized portion of spice-rubbed beef tenderloin, served with chicken and chorizo sausage, Argentine-style.

Sushi also finds a place here, along with oyster shooters and a list of tacos. In fact, what doesn't? The menu lists guinea pig as a teaser (we think).

It borders on insanity even to dream of desserts to follow these mammoth portions, but dream on: The tres leches cake serves eight, and the key lime sorbet is properly zingy.

The drinks list is just as forward, ranging from Hot Zone beers, sakes, and flights of rum to retro cocktails, along with Ting and Inca Cola for those dreaming of Jamaica and Peru.

In summertime, the French windows facing the street are thrown open, inviting repartee with the passing parade.

CHRISTOS

2632 Nicollet Avenue South, Minneapolis
(612) 871-2111

Union Depot Place, 214 Fourth Street East, Saint Paul
(651) 224-6000 • www.christos.com
$$; P

GREEKS WERE BORN to be hospitable—at least, if Gus and Carol Parpas are any indication. Walking into their Eat Street restaurant is like entering their home, except it holds a lot more tables. Smiles prevail as you're seated in this cheery, bright room reminiscent of the islands—all white and blue and splashed with sunshine. Below the expansive, many-paned windows looking out onto Nicollet, green plants flourish on a ledge, soaking up the rays. Those tables, dressed in crisp, white linen, have been known to get pushed against the walls for an impromptu circle of swaying dancers in response to strands of bouzouki music. And, of course, salutes of "Opa!" resonate whenever the kitchen (visible in the rear) sends out a plate of saganaki, the Greek flaming-cheese dish that's doused with dramatic flair at tableside.

All the classic Greek appetizers are found on the menu, toned by Gus's Cypriot palate. Choose spreads and dips such as hummus; tzatziki (yogurt laced with cucumbers, dill, and garlic); melintzanosalata—a puree of roasted eggplant with more of that aromatic garlic; skordalia—garlic laced with potatoes, although it's the other way around on the menu description; or a mixed platter, accompanied by toasted rounds of pita bread.

Hot appetizers include that celebratory saganaki, a spicy grilled sausage, and octopus baked with onions, red wine, and bay leaf. Kindly, Gus also serves

MAUD BORUP CHOCOLATIER

Calhoun Square • 3001 Hennepin Avenue South
Minneapolis • (612) 827-2203

The shop is new but the name is a local classic. The original Maud Borup chocolate store in downtown Saint Paul is long gone, but the tradition of offering finely crafted chocolates continues in the Calhoun Square location. The shop displays cases of top-quality candies, from chocolate cashew turtles to fudge balls and key lime truffles, as well as a menu of designer chocolate drinks that includes chai cocoa and the popular "Uptown" number: dark chocolate, espresso, and hazelnut flavoring. The store also hosts kids' parties and showers. Chocolate-related giftware is featured here, too.

several of his standout entrées in appetizer portions: spanakopita, souvlaki skewers, stuffed grape leaves, gyros, moussaka (including a vegetarian version), and pastitsio, a macaroni-based casserole.

Avgolemono is the favored soup, rich with egg and spritzed with lemon. Both Greek and tabouli salads head the list of greens. Dinner entrées, which include soup or salad, lead off with a roll call of traditional favorites, including the Cypriot version of stuffed grape leaves and some not-so-traditional inventions, such as the gyros salad—a Greek salad topped with leaves of roasted meat. Lamb is the specialty of the kitchen, served as shish kebab, lemon-marinated chops, and a tender, long-baked shank bathed in a rich sauce of dill and caramelized onions. Oregano chicken, shrimp Mykonos, and pork souvlaki fill in the cracks. But the best bet is to order one of the half-dozen sampler plates, which offer tastes of three delicacies. A list of Greek wines and beers adds to the exuberant experience.

Baklava, plump with walnuts and honey, proves the most popular dessert, but rice pudding and an inventive combination of apples and ricotta baked in phyllo have found their following, too. Add a dark, thick Greek coffee to achieve complete authenticity. Or shatter a plate against the wall.

FAMOUS DAVE'S BBQ AND BLUES

Calhoun Square, 3001 Hennepin Avenue South, Minneapolis
(612) 822-9900 • www.famousdaves.com
14 metro locations
$$; F; M

DAVE'S FAMOUS? No, no no. When Dave Anderson decided to bring his home cooking to market in the early 90s, he didn't want a forgettable title like that. So he reversed the wording—and, what do you know?—the sentiment proved true. Dave has become justly famous not only as a Wisconsin-born Native American making good on his family's recipes for barbecue but also, more recently, as appointee in the role of U.S. Secretary of Indian Affairs. And he's also grown his original enterprise to 14 Twin Cities locations as well to numerous places throughout the rest of Minnesota and, indeed, across the nation.

The Calhoun Square venue is the flagship of the endeavor, bringing that magic mix of funky barbecue and blues to the city's hub of singles' action, backed by plenty of suburban shoppers hungry for a taste of smoke as well as neighborhood families who'd rather let Dave and crew do it up right than mess with the grill at home.

Follow the music (live every evening after 9 p.m.) to the center of Calhoun Square. From there on, the aroma will guide you. The sprawling joint itself, comfortably dim, with well-worn, no-frills wooden tables and heavy beams above a concrete floor, draws character from the old 33 rpm albums on the walls and vintage neon signs—a guitar and a gas station's flying horse amid the blazing beer logos. TV monitors flicker behind the spacious bar, and a stage-cum-dance floor featuring class acts steps up the pulse as the night gets late and later.

The secret Dave divulges is giving his signature meats a rubdown with his special blend of herbs and spices, then slow-smoking the cuts over a smoldering hickory fire for up to nine hours. (Who but Dave would have that kind of patience?) Just before serving, the meats are sent under the grill for a light charring to seal in the juices and caramelize the rich coating of Dave's own barbecue sauce. Purists, who like their spareribs sans sauce, just need to ask to have them "naked."

Those Saint Louis–style bones come in several sizes, à la carte or served up on a platter with a cornbread muffin, corn on the cob, and your choice of two more sides, including coleslaw, drunken apples, baked beans, fries, and potato salad. Accommodating as he is, Dave also offers lots of combo plates, involving variations on the theme of ribs: with brisket, chopped pork, double-smoked ham, or chicken. All of the above come in sandwich portions, too.

If you've got an appetite that takes no prisoners, start off with a pile of chicken wings or catfish fingers, a bowl of chicken wild rice soup, or a Caesar salad.

"Seize the moment; diet tomorrow" is a saying Dave flaunts when customers moan at the very mention of dessert. But it would be a pity to miss his sweet bread pudding, or what he claims is "better than mom's" pecan pie.

Kids' meals and family to-go portions are popular options, too.

FIGLIO

3001 Hennepin Avenue South, Calhoun Square, Minneapolis
(612) 822-1688 • figlio.com
$$; O

FIGLIO COMMANDS A LOCATION that many a rival restaurateur would kill for. Its parent company, the Parasole Corporation, did its homework well; the café anchors the corner of Hennepin and Lake in Calhoun Square, with the highest auto, bus, and foot-traffic count in the twin towns. By offering its extensive Cal-Ital menu in two settings, it serves two diverse audiences well.

A bar, with "greenhouse" glass windows onto the street scene and sidewalk seating in the summer months, appeals to the area's dense population of trendy singles, who can circulate around the freestanding bar itself. In the dining room behind it, warmed with wood walls and crisp, white tablecloths, a quieter, clublike atmosphere draws Kenwood's more mature empty-nesters, especially before or after a nearby movie. This is the best of both worlds. The same menu serves both scenes, produced by an open kitchen in the rear from which flames leap forth with the regularity of Old Faithful.

Billboards, with a single catchy word in neon pink—bruschetta, spiedini, cavatappi—pique diners' curiosity. Chances are, the award-winning wood-oven pizzas they already know. Word of mouth spreads fast when they're this well prepared. Built on a base of hand-tossed crust or ultra-slim cracker, they walk the fine line between customary and crazed—neither dull nor nutty. Favorites roam from the traditional margherita with tomato sauce and mozzarella to the inventive combo of roasted squash, Italian sausage, and caramelized onions.

Pastas toe the same fine line. Guests may enjoy a simple, well-made spaghetti Napoletana or opt for the cavatappi, piled with grilled chicken, kalamatas, sun dried tomatoes, feta, and a hit of hot red pepper. The tortellini on which to blow your diet have been a star of the menu since day one, sauced with butter, cream, and Parmesan, then studded with peas, mushrooms, and prosciutto. Nor are the salads to be overlooked, particularly the gutsy Caesar.

These days the list leads off with tasting plates, such as salmon with warm lentil salad or crisp-fried bluepoint oysters with spinach-artichoke pesto and caviar cream. A trio of soups banishes the bane of the undecided with sips of saffron bisque, pea soup with truffle oil, and a potage of roasted sweet red peppers.

The wood-fired oven spitting flames is the force behind oven-roasted meats, such as the house-brined Iowa pork chop, a porterhouse, or those spiedini—skewers of choice beef tenderloin steeped in Bardolino wine.

Meals begin with a basket of chunky, rustic bread and a splash of olive oil poured into each diner's saucer by the tuned-in servers, who seem to love their duties. Feasts end, for those still left standing, with a mile-high, many-layered chocolate cake drizzled with yet more chocolate.

Figlio's martinis have tongues wagging; these days the house also infuses its own specialty vodkas. The wine list offers many a good selection by the glass, quartino (a glass and a half), and bottle, allowing for experimentation. Best time to get adventurous is during the dual happy hours the bar offers from 4 to 7 p.m. and again after 10 p.m., with many drink and snacking specials.

FRENCH MEADOW CAFÉ AND BAKERY

2610 Lyndale Avenue South, Minneapolis
(612) 870-7855 • frenchmeadow.com
$–$$; P; F; O

JUST LIKE THE PEACENIKS of the 70s, the once-funky French Meadow has tempered its zealous "alternative" mission over the years in tandem with the evolving, ever-broader, more sophisticated tastes of its clientele, who now are just as likely to own Beamers as Schwinns and have traded up their knapsacks for briefcases. What started as a missionary enclave for healthier-than-thou baked goods and light vegetarian provender ordered at a counter now includes evening table service, a list of interesting beers and wines, and a menu that can compete for variety and intrigue with many a leading bistro's—which, these days, is what French Meadow is.

ISLES BUN & COFFEE

1424 West 28th Street • Minneapolis • (612) 870-4466

The shop is smaller than your average closet—but far more aromatic—while the buns it produces will feed a family of four. There are two ways to enjoy the yeasty treats: pinwheeled with cinnamon, with a bowl of frosting to scoop over the top according to the dictates of your conscience, or topped with seductively sticky caramel and pecans. Because the shop sells great o.j. and coffee, too, it's almost become a traffic hazard as devotees pull over on their way to work. Weekend mornings, eager supplicants cram the floor space and lines trail out the door to the scattering of sidewalk tables. These days, the blackboard menu lists scones and killer cookies, too.

Where's the beef? Not here, but who needs it? The kitchen has broadened its outlook to include seafood and poultry among its dining options (vegans, not to worry: You'll still find many dishes to your taste) while keeping to the establishment's original philosophy of presenting seasonal, local, and organically grown ingredients.

The décor has undergone a subtle upgrade, too. The scattering of tables beneath the high ceiling today sport votive candles and tastefully arranged posies. Menus are now available to back up the lofty blackboards with their lists. In the summertime, sidewalk seats are clustered beneath the café's signature green awning, sheltered from street-side traffic by planters adrift with wildflowers.

What hasn't changed—and let's hope it never will—is the bakery counter's show-and-tell display of treats to sustain you in great style from breakfast on through dinner, to enjoy here or available to go. Apple streusel muffins and white chocolate-cranberry scones vie with Minnesota wild-rice cakes as morning fare, backed by cookies (low fat or full strength), carrot cake, elaborate tortes, and impossible-to-resist cheesecakes, as well as a litany of country-style loaves.

Heartier breakfast choices range from blueberry corn pancakes or sourdough French toast to eggs with smoked salmon, breakfast quiches, burritos, huevos rancheros, or a killer Benedict glossed with the kitchen's signature watercress hollandaise.

Lunch fare runs the gamut from a choice of a half-dozen soups and organic salads, including favorites like Cobb, Niçoise, and Caesar, to black bean crab cakes with a zippy chipotle-garlic aioli, global noodle numbers, a vegetarian shepherd's pie crowned with garlic-laced mashed potatoes and snappy cheddar, and a dozen lusty sandwiches.

Dinner entrées include paprika-roasted free-range chicken with lemongrass-chive pesto; salmon glazed with miso; trout from Star Prairie, Wisconsin; and a vegan rosemary polenta cake lavished with roasted vegetables. Oh, and did we mention those desserts winking at you from the counter? Add an espresso and purr all the way home.

FUJI YA

600 West Lake Street, Minneapolis
(612) 871-4055 • fujiyasushi.com
$$; P

THE LANDMARK FUJI YA opened in 1959, the first Japanese restaurant in the Twin Cities. The concept proved so popular that Reiko Weston, a college student, left school to help her mother run her restaurant. In the 60s Reiko took over ownership and moved the restaurant to the banks of the Mississippi—a serene riverside setting designed with subtle artistry, where she went on to introduce local diners to the lively, interactive teppanyaki style of cooking, and in the early 80s she added the cities' first sushi bar.

The riverfront restaurant closed its doors upon Reiko's untimely death. But in 2001 her daughter, Carol, and her husband, Tom Hanson, decided to continue the legacy. They launched the new Fuji Ya in the trendy Lyn-Lake neighborhood, home of alternative arts and a crowd who lives for sushi.

The café captures the best of old and new. Carol saved her mother's Japanese woodcuts and the futsuma—gold-paneled doors—from the former site, which now grace the walls of the new restaurant. A bamboo fountain at the entrance brings back memories of the old restaurant as well.

In the dining room, abstract metal bamboo trees, a generous use of wood, and a black-slate path winding through the dining room to the copper fountain impart the feel of a Japanese garden.

The bar has a more modern feel, from its shiny gold booths to the sparkling metallic gold on the concrete floor, which Carol likes to call her "Las Vegas–style" look. A semicircular sushi bar seating 20 serves as a stage setting for four sushi chefs, who nimbly conjure choice ingredients into nearly 40 varieties of the art form, highlighted by a blackboard list of daily specials.

Carol's menu represents the classic Japanese preparations by which the Fuji Ya earned its fame: tempura, teriyaki, and noodle dishes. Augmenting the list of sushi and sashimi, the appetizer fare leads off with yakitori—skewers of grilled chicken; harumaki, a Japanese-style egg roll; seaweed salad; and tataki, a.k.a. carpaccio of beef and tuna, served with a savory ponzu dipping sauce.

Entrées include a warming portion of miso soup as well as a house salad and rice. Yose nabe is a heavenly meal in a bowl—shrimp, mussels, cod, salmon, and chicken tossed with tofu, vegetables, Japanese mushrooms, and noodles—while sukiyaki, made from Carol's traditional family recipe, salutes a soup-stew of beef, vegetables, and noodles in a savory broth. Bowls of udon or soba noodles are adaptable to add-ons like shrimp or vegetable tempura or rib eye of beef. And beef is also offered grilled, Kobe-style.

Desserts may not be routine in the restaurants of Japan, but Carol has come up with tradition-based finales to satisfy a local palate craving sweets. Ice creams, made to order by the local Sonny's firm, include green tea and ginger; they're also available in a fire-and-ice tempura style. Or summon the ginger scoop served with plum wine. The restaurant also boasts a fine list of sakes and Japanese beers.

GIORGIO'S

2451 Hennepin Avenue South, Minneapolis
(612) 374-5131
$$; P; O

THINK BACK TO the late 70s. If you were old enough to fill a booster chair in an Italian restaurant around these parts, you had two choices: spaghetti with red sauce or red sauce on pizza. We're talking long before the days when tasty treats like pesto and focaccia made their way from northern Italy to become household words in the northland of Minnesota.

Giorgio Cherubini is the one who set us straight. Born in Florence as the youngest of *una famiglia molto grande* that managed a pasta factory, he grew up knowing that good eating was not only an art form but also a birthright. He recalls holidays on the Tuscan farmstead where his aunt taught him all she knew about cooking, from testing an oven's heat with her hand before the bread went in to preparing wedding feasts for 300 family members— "catering," laughs Giorgio today, although back then it was simply part of a day's routine.

The quest for an engineering degree brought him to America, where he worked in the then–Northstar Hotel's fine dining room to help pay tuition. As the years slid by, the dual tugs on his time drove him *pazzo*—crazy—so the moment of decision came and he traded his slide rule for a spatula.

His first restaurant, Hosteria Fiorentina, which opened in 1987, took foodies' palates by storm. After it fell to the wrecking ball, he opened Giorgio's on Hennepin in 1980 and another at 50th and France in 1996 (since closed).

"I was one of the few chef-owners at the time," Giorgio recalls of the daring launch. "I introduced authentic Tuscan food. I made my own bread and used it for focaccia, bruschetta, ribollita [bread soup]. I still do; I believe in it."

He also introduced Twin Cities diners to some new things: the concept of olive oil for dipping that crusty loaf; his signature wild boar pasta ragu; and the idea of dining in courses, the way Italians do—first an antipasto, such as his fabulous roasted beets scattered with nuts and Gorgonzola, then a pasta course, a lusty entrée (he offers three choices nightly—a meat, a fish, and a fowl), followed by a sweet such as the cake he's named after his daughter, Francesca, ending with an espresso. And, of course, there's a long list of fine Italian wines to enhance the experience.

The trattoria's setting is so intimate—well, crowded—that you may get to know your neighbors pretty well; that's part of the pleasure of grabbing a chair here. The atmosphere may not be fancy, but it's livened with sophisticated take-offs of museum art and other quirky touches that oversee dishes such as his famous Caesar salad, in which garlic reigns, and sweet, squash-stuffed pillows of ravioli, lazing in a brown butter sauce. Splitting portions with a companion is a vice indulged in by many who want it all but without popping buttons, and the indulgent staff is glad to accommodate.

IT'S GREEK TO ME

626 West Lake Street, Minneapolis
(612) 825-9922
$$; F; O

AHEAD OF ITS TIME, for decades It's Greek to Me has anchored the newly hot Lake and Lyndale intersection, luring lovers of gyros and moussaka from all corners of the metro long before Lyn-Lake accumulated its critical mass of ethnic eateries, offbeat theater, and upstart boutiques that's fueled its trendy-destination status.

In recent years, an inviting garden patio has taken shape, where diners defy the hum of passing traffic and relax beneath a leafy arbor, pretending their toes are warmed by the sands of the islands. Not much else has changed in the café's

BILL'S IMPORTED FOODS

721 West Lake Street • Minneapolis • (612) 827-2891

The blue awning with its Greek key design etched in white signals to devotees of fine Mediterranean foodstuffs that they're arrived at the Olympus of local markets. Step in, and the basket of flatbreads at the door offers fragrant reassurance that you've found the right place. Aside tins of olive oil in XXL sizes stand pyramids of canned tomatoes, broad beans, artichokes, eggplant, you name it. Down one aisle, sacks of rice boast origins in Italy, India, and Egypt. Shelves groan with cuts of Greek cheeses, from feta to kasseri, as well as cartons of tabouli, tzatziki, tart yogurt, sweet halvah, and baklava. In the cooler, coils of Greek sausages beckon, along with goat, rabbit, and lamb. Olives glisten in the deli case, beside fresh produce and dried fruits and nuts galore. Grape leaves are prerolled with tasty stuffings, and phyllo comes already fashioned into pastries to make party-giving easy.

formula for success. Enter, past the deli counter of treats to go, backed by the firing line of working ranges, and the tongue you hear from those cooks on duty is Greek. And many in the cities' Greek community consider nowhere else when it's time to celebrate a birthday, wedding, or any other excuse to gather the extended family. But those who cannot claim that heritage and whose language skills are limited to "Opa!" also have been quick to adopt this city-side taverna as their home.

Inside the closely pulled wooden shutters that keep the intersection's activities at bay, spare white walls and seating nooks recreate the flavor of the homeland. As does the menu.

It's extensive. And it's authentic, starting with the attractive list of mezedes to whet your appetite. Taramosalata, melitzanosalata, skordalia, and tzatziki form the quartet of the classic Greek spreads and dips to enjoy with warm rounds of pita, perhaps with a side of rice-stuffed grape leaves. Saganaki, the golden-brown plate of molten cheese, draws those hoots of "Opa!" when it's ignited tableside, perhaps accompanied by a slice of spanakopita, the phyllo-crusted cheese and spinach pie, or links of homemade Greek sausage or shrimp in a winey mustard sauce. Several combination plates relieve the burden of decision-making for those who cannot bear to leave a delicacy untried.

Of course there's a Greek salad, lush with lemon-green peppers, purple olives, and chalk-white cubes of feta cheese. Avgolemono is the standout soup among a trio offered, spiked with a wake-up shot of lemon to balance its rich, creamy nature.

Entrées, be warned, are not nouvelle in portion size. Come famished or prepare to carry home a doggie bag. Roast leg of lamb leads the list, or choose the meat in tender cubes, stewed with wine and tomatoes. The kitchen's gyros plate mixes beef and lamb, while comforting "hot dishes," as we in Minnesota are prone to say, include moussaka and pastitsio, just like the fare in Athens.

Souvlakia—kebabs—please the meat eaters, who also partake of chops, steaks, and Greek-style chicken, marinated in lemon, olive oil, and oregano. Shrimp Santorini blends tomato, feta, and onions with the broiled shellfish.

The baklava is homemade here, bursting with chopped nuts, cinnamon, and sugar, oozing with honeyed syrup. Kadafai, just a touch lighter, is another option, as is the phyllo-wrapped custard called galaktobouriko. Or choose the creamy rice pudding before you have a tiny cup of thick, ink-black Greek coffee.

Greek wines join more familiar labels on the list, presented by sweet young servers who refuse to hurry the merry tables whiling away the minutes with lively talk.

JP AMERICAN BISTRO

2937 Lyndale Avenue South, Minneapolis
(612) 824-9300 • jpamericanbistro.com
$$; O; P

TWIN CITIES DINERS are nothing if not patient. Since J. P. Samuelson entered the food scene, they've worshiped his cooking, but after left his post as exec chef at D'Amico Cucina, one of the area's most haute of all haute kitchens, it was two years before he opened the bistro of his dreams. Today these fans are gratefully tucking napkins under their chins once again—this time to catch the robust sauces from his foray into more casual, everyday fare, built on the techniques and inspired combinations that were formerly his forte.

Those two years were spent foraging for financial aid, securing a suitable space and refurbishing it, and shoring up the bank loans and investors' help with sweat equity. Passersby at night could spot J. P. in his new digs in the hip and artsy Lyn-Lake neighborhood, next door to the similarly new and arts-

DUC LOI INTERNATIONAL MARKET

2429 Nicollet Avenue • Minneapolis • (612) 874-0913

It's one-stop shopping in this vast Asian market, which is clean, well lit, yet the antithesis of fancy. And that's what keeps the prices so modest—that, and a steady stream of Asian customers who see no reason to pay for overhead. While the interior shelves are bursting with Asian staples such as noodles, sauces, coconut milk, pickles, and other canned and bottled goods, the perimeter is dedicated to fresh herbs, fruits, and vegetables, from longbeans to green mango, baby bok choy, bamboo shoots, and potent peppers (even smelly durian, that daunting fruit), plus a myriad of flavorful herbs, starting with potato leaves and ending with stems of lemongrass.

In the fish and meat counter, goat is promoted, along with chicken feet, pigs' heads, and, to many Euro-bred shoppers, many more unfamiliar meats and fishes, all at bargain prices. The freezer cases are loaded with the likes of dim sum buns, longan fruit, jackfruit, bean cakes, and cassava, as well as Vietnamese sausages and seafood. And the owner cheerfully chats up whomever he's serving at the checkout counter.

forward Jungle Theater. There he was, swinging a paintbrush and sawing lumber under a hanging light bulb, working right up until that long-awaited opening night in 2003.

Today the café sports newly exposed beams and utilitarian ducts-turned-decor above walls of cement blocks swabbed in hues of chocolate and oatmeal. They're accented by panels of glass brick that form the minimalist backdrop for the open kitchen in the rear—the real design statement of the place, and epicenter of the action.

Most nights, J. P. can be seen stirring sauces, manning the sauté pan, and garnishing plates to speed them to diners salivating for his signature thin-crust pizzas, gingery calamari in a Thai dipping sauce, and warm salad of duck confit—fitting starters to an entrée list headed by diver scallops partnered with roasted beets atop a drizzle of chive oil and potent glowing nuggets of wasabi.

Yet diners have been known to order simply comfort food, and welcome to it—a bowl of soup, green salad, and scoop of mashed potatoes. In winter, J. P. likes to pair pork tenderloin with diced apple and toasted chestnuts on a pillow of polenta, while in spring, when ramps are just uncurling and morels are in their prime, he showcases them on a plate of fresh halibut.

The bread here is dense and delicious, only outdone by the desserts. It's easy to inhale a chocolate-mole cake hopping with pasilla chiles, tamarind glaze, and orange caramel.

Who's the pretty hostess that answers the phone? It's J. P.'s wife. And the rest of the staff is equally accommodating. They'll seat livelier groups in the street-front bar, where the full menu and enticing wine list are always available, while before- or after-theater parties may prefer the chance to hash over the evening's drama in the quieter dining room. That way they're sure to catch the drama at the open kitchen, too.

LA BODEGA

3005 Lyndale Avenue South, Minneapolis
(612) 823-2661
$-$$; O; M

HABLA TAPAS? Blessedly, anyone can speak that language fluently in Minneapolis, thanks to the lively little Spanish restaurant that opened in April 2000, bringing that appealing Spanish dining concept our way. And the Lyn-Lake intersection, heartbeat of the town's neo-Bohemia, makes the perfect setting for the convivial grazing concept that's all the dining rage. A bodega is a casual wine bar in the homeland, and "tapas" mean "small plates"; that's all the Spanish language you need to know to feel immediately at home here.

The tiny storefront (there's an actual restaurant attached on the corner, operated by the same owners, which offers a more conventional dining experience) is crammed with rustic, handmade wooden tables and heavy, farmhouse-style chairs to match, crowded against walls of a pungent mustard hue showcasing atmospheric black-and-white photographs capturing café life in Spain. A wine bar, lined in bright imported tiles, helps set the stage for Spanish nibbles to be shared with friends and an evening of animated conversation.

La Bodega's extensive listing of little plates is divided into three categories: vegetarian, seafood, and meat—some hot, some cold, and all for sharing. Classic vegetable compositions from Andalucia include a Spanish-style tortilla of onions and potatoes, rather like a slice of quiche. Or dive into patatas aioli, a heap of roasted spuds slathered with a garlicky mayonnaise sauce. To cool off a sultry summer evening, try gazpacho, the refreshing chilled soup, white asparagus dressed in olive oil and vinegar, or simply a handful of Mediterranean olives of various pedigrees. Grilled eggplant tossed with zucchini and sweet red peppers or a golden molten square of fried Manchego cheese painted with tomato sauce make hearty winter starters.

Seafood tapas swim readily from the kitchen, starting with the Spanish favorite, grilled garlic shrimp; then on to clams sauced in olive oil, garlic, and white wine; a carpaccio of tuna; halibut croquettes; or a taste of paella, starring mixed bits of seafood atop aromatic saffron rice.

Chorizo, served on polenta or in a tortilla omelet, shines among the lusty meat selections; as do the thin, pungent slices of prosciutto; pork tenderloin roasted with rosemary; Spanish meatballs in a rich tomato sauce; and whole roasted quail.

Yes, there's dessert, but in true Spanish style, they're afterthoughts: ice cream, a tiramisu that sneaked by the border guard, and a supple, custardy flan. Beer, wine, sherries, and sangria are on hand to accent the tasty morsels. And on weekends, the tiny stage in the rear, backed by silhouettes of dancers painted on the wall, comes alive with the seductive, insistent rhythms of flamenco as a guitarist and dancers open their souls.

LUCIA'S

1432 West 31st Street, Minneapolis
(612) 825-1572 • lucias.com
$$; O; P

THEY CALL LUCIA WATSON the Alice Waters of Minnesota because, like her idol based in San Francisco, she's passionately dedicated to serving a simple menu of spanking-fresh regional food at modest prices.

Lucia opened her eponymous Uptown café in 1985, building on her catering experience at the Minnetonka Art Center. "I was at the point where I had to decide to invest in more trucks and equipment or do something else," she explains. "I noticed this location and decided it would be better for people to come here rather than have me haul to clients' homes."

And Uptowners are delighted to accommodate her. Since then, she's doubled her space, added a wine bar, and grown her staff from 13 to 50. Wisely, she's remained true to her mission. Procurers of processed ingredients can't get through the kitchen door. Yet the neighborhood's starving artists can find a spectacular bowl of soup and bread—slices of chewy French loaves, which are the forte of the kitchen's ovens—and still get change from a $5 bill.

They're probably rubbing elbows with arts funders and corporate CEOs at adjoining tables, for Lucia attracts a diverse but knowing clientele. The common denominator is an appreciation of tasty but ungussied dishes that allow the best of fresh ingredients to sing for themselves, such as baked Wisconsin trout with roasted potatoes and green beans, or perhaps chicken braised with tomatoes, garlic, and herbs, sent out over egg noodles. Diners choose from a list kept short but changed often—simply a meat, a poultry item, a fish, and a vegetarian specialty.

Lunchers can always find a hearty salad such as the farmer's mix of field greens tossed with blue cheese, spiced pecans, bacon, and craisins in a maple-mustard vinaigrette, backed by an omelet or sandwich and something more substantial, like a pot pie or a stew. And this is one restaurant where it's wise to heed a server's invitation to save room for dessert—from pound cake to profiteroles, they're terrific.

Lucia's sunny storefront setting maintains the same sort of simplicity—bare blond floors, uncluttered walls of sparkling white, and tables set with nosegays. At night, petite votive candles abet the low, romantic lighting. True to her palate, Lucia's wine list shows the same good taste as her menus.

LUCIA WATSON

Lucia's Restaurant

Chef Lucia Watson is a trailblazer on the trail of fresh, often organic, and always unprocessed provender on the local scene. Putting her money (or market share) where her mouth is, she serves such fare on her restaurant's menu by getting to know local farmers and their wares. But in her commitment to the cause, she also devotes time to teaching others this value. She has joined the Land Stewardship Council, "where we talk about how we can make this work better." She serves on the Organic Advisory Task Force established by Minnesota's Commissioner of Agriculture. And she chairs the Youth Farm Marketing Project, which teaches inner-city kids job skills and work ethics through the medium of garden work. Spreading the gospel even further afield, Lucia also has written a popular cookbook and regularly contributes to national culinary magazines.

The adjoining wine bar—the first in a city where it's now become a buzz-word concept—is a bit more whimsical in its intimate space, with daily "finds" showcased on a blackboard hung behind the counter, bistro-style. For those who yearn to investigate a retinue of unfamiliar labels, Lucia offers many half-glass portions. Interesting microbrews also win a place in the lineup, as does a recent addition of cocktails to her list. Nightly, the wine bar draws couples who treasure the opportunity for quiet conversation, away from the hubbub of Uptown's cruisers and jam-packed bars. Snacks, such as cheese plates, sandwiches, and fabulous desserts, are available on this side of the doorway, too.

MORELOS MEX GRILL

14 West 26th Street, Minneapolis
(612) 870-0053

2 West 66th Street, Richfield
(612) 243-9699
$; F

HERE'S A SUCCESS STORY it's been heartwarming to observe—and, of course, the observation required enjoying many a meal over a span of years. When first the restaurant opened as Tacos Morelos, the founder, a recent arrival from Mexico, took over a hole in the wall just off Eat Street and, with the able assistance of his Spanish-speaking staff, cooked for his compadres in the emerging Hispanic neighborhood, as well as for the fortunate gringos who happened in and spread the word.

Today the original site has expanded threefold. It shimmers as a snappy cantina, featuring a tin ceiling and walls in tones of lime-green and tortilla-tan, hung with kitschy artifacts—sombreros, saddles, saws, and brass mariachi instruments—that accent the brightly striped curtains on the windows. A shrine to the Virgin faces off with a mural of a mustachioed Zapata, and lively Mexican music fills the space. Rush-seated chairs facing butcher-block tables are filled with locals—students, laborers, and business folk in happy cohabitation—all hours of the day, waiting for the sunny servers, who now speak English, albeit with a charming lilt to the language, to pile the tables with whatever smells so good in the kitchen.

The menu is nothing exceptional—a familiar list of appetizers, soups, a taco salad, and a Cuban torta as the sandwich offering, plus enchiladas, burritos, and such favoring a variety of meats including chicken, pork, beef, chorizo, shellfish, and plenty for vegetarians to savor. But the flavors are fresh and vibrant, clearly homemade rather than from a package or a can. In fact, catch a glimpse of the cooks in the rear as they cause the flames to jump on the griddle, and one is all the more motivated to order the molcajeto de carne, delivered in a hot stone bowl: ranchero cheese and two salsas smothering carne asada, chorizo, chicken, peppers, onions, and nopales (those flat, green cactus leaves), enough for a party of four. Or choose the seafood version.

House specialties range from chili rellenos to coctel de camarones (shrimp cocktail, South of the Border–style). Start off with dainty, chicken-filled flautas, a burnished quesadilla, or a bowl of menudo, the classic tripe stew that many Mexicans swear by. End the meal, if you're still upright, with flan, arroz con leche (creamy rice pudding), or helados (gelato to Italians) bathed in chocolate sauce.

The new iteration of the restaurant, which has opened a second location in Richfield, includes a minuscule bar, whose empty cervesa bottles now house salt and pepper on the tables and tequila quarts serve as flower vases. Not only are margaritas and Mexican beers favored now that a liquor license has been secured, but a library of 20 tequilas seizes top billing. Sidewalk tables, fashioned of bright tiles, anchor the sidewalk in the summer, another nice addition. And all the more reason to holler, "Ole!"

PIZZA LUCE

3200 Lyndale Avenue South, Minneapolis
(612) 827-5978

119 North Fourth Street, Minneapolis
(612) 333-7359

2200 East Franklin Avenue, Minneapolis
(612) 332-2534 • pizzaluce.com
$; P

COME FOR THE PIZZA, stay for the vibes. Both the long-lived Warehouse District and Lyn-Lake venues that serve as magnets for the arts and counter-culture crowd, and now a third café in the neo-hip Seward neighborhood, are playgrounds for the antiestablishment. And Luce's staff, dressed in regimental black—except, of course, for the occasional lime green Mohawk or day-glo tattoo—set the pace. The mood is happening but mellow, from the steady lunch trade on through dinner to late night and into the early morning.

Lounging in the back wall of booths or ringing the rows of tables, gaggles of Gen Xers—waiters on their days off, the next new wave of musicians, what have you—share beer, pizza, and opinions. Oh, the suits troop in steadily as well, but many in the briefcase and cell phone crowd opt for takeout. The delivery phone rings madly at all hours, too.

The Uptown parking lot is always full, another good sign that the product is primo and the price is right. Pizza Luce's counter personnel are an upbeat bunch, and the crew in the open work area behind them (this is not a hoity-toity demo kitchen) is on the move. They prep crusts composed of whole-grain flour and olive oil and give them a generous topping of quality mozzarella plus your choice of white sauce, laced with enough garlic to combat whatever ails you, or red sauce, which accounts for the gallon tomato cans stacked in pyramids like paint buckets against the front window.

For specialty toppings, the choice is yours: Go with one of the dozen or so house concoctions, including the Maximum that begins with homemade Italian sausage and ends eight ingredients later, or the baked potato pizza, with mashed baby reds topped with broccoli, tomatoes, cheddar, and bacon. Vegetarians rate another dozen composed creations of their own. Or construct a pie from the list of 50 toppings.

Hoagies float out the door pretty fast, too, as do salads for "in" or to go, and hot pasta numbers that include a lasagna verdant with spinach as well as the Abruzzi version, with homemade sausage, four cheeses, and Luce's own basil-tomato sauce. Yes, there are apps if you're really ravenous—focaccia to chicken wings to ramekins of artichoke dip—and desserts: carrot cake, cheesecake, tiramisu, and Rice Krispie bars as big as a small child's head.

The warm, brown cocoon of the Uptown venue boasts a plate rail lined with bottles of Italian wine, a suggestive sell that works for me. Beer and soft drinks also grace many a table.

RAINBOW CHINESE RESTAURANT

2739 Nicollet Avenue South, Minneapolis
(612) 870-7084 • rainbowrestaurant.com
$–$$; P: F

THE RAINBOW KEEPS its promise. Diners following it to Eat Street come away rewarded with the culinary equivalent of that proverbial pot of gold: authentic Asian cooking presented in an inviting, contemporary setting that's almost as fashion-forward as the trendy neighborhood artistes, literati, and politicos who fill its 80 seats. They mingle regularly with minivans of aficionados from the suburbs and Jewish fans from all over, who particularly appreciate heading here on Christmas Eve. (It's one of the few nice places open.)

The restaurant was launched quietly back in 1983, when the Wong family arrived as refugees from a Chinese enclave in Vietnam. Their patriarch bought the humble café to support his nine children, all immediately drafted into service in one capacity or another. Dad cooked. Daughter Tammy, then 20, who spoke English, took over the business management and, as time passed, assumed ownership.

In the late 90s, she moved the Rainbow to bigger, better quarters just across the street. By then, word had spread and it had become a destination for more than the neighborhood's Asians, addicted to its noodle dishes and other traditional, homey fare seldom found on other local menus. Hotel concierges sent Asians in town on business to her kitchen, and newspaper reviewers directed the rest of the metro to Tammy's door (an attractive set of French doors, actually, which she unearthed in a vintage restoration shop and painted red and gold, set off with some attractive stained glass and other artistic touches).

Although she boasts no formal culinary training, she's cooked forever. Tammy oversees the Rainbow's extensive menu, which includes some street-vendor favorites she learned to love in Vietnam and classic dishes from cafés in Hong Kong, where she worked as a kid. The most popular item, along with those noodles, is a whole fried walleye presented in black bean sauce.

Although they don't show up on her takeout menu, Tammy is delighted to prepare typical home-cookin' dishes like winter melon soup, oyster pancakes, pickled mustard greens, and congee for adventurers seeking the seductive street flavors of Asia. To accommodate her more mainstream clientele, Tammy offers her take on the standards, too: kung pao chicken, a spicy chicken satay with asparagus, Hunan beef with chilies, a milder moo shu pork, and the popular Szechuan-style shrimp with sweet bell peppers playing against spicy black peppercorns.

Chiu Chao rice cakes, a south China favorite, come fried with turnips or taro; green beans are sautéed with garlic and bits of preserved cabbage; and Chinese eggplant joins garlic in a spicy ginger sauce, all pleasing to vegetarians as well, along with an endless list of her house special, pan-fried noodles. Choose them Hong Kong–style—flat and wide, rich with eggs; thin Chow Mai Fun noodles or their fat Chow Fun cousins; slender strands called Hor Fun, made from rice; or round wheat skeins of lo mein. Many diners simply stop in for a huge, comforting bowl of noodle soup with whatever protein they may fancy, from a medley of shrimp, squid, and fish cake to roast duck, beef brisket, or barbecued pork.

Special round-table dinners and, of course, multicourse feasts for Chinese New Year allow Tammy to orchestrate complementary menus that show off her kitchen at its best.

TRYG'S

3118 West Lake Street, Minneapolis
(612) 920-7777
$$; P; O

TRYG'S OPENED in late 2004, just in time to charm holiday revelers who had heard about the new star blazing on the dining circuit. Thanks to the conscientious homework by owner Tryg Truelson, the parking valets can fund a college education. (They're already well schooled in hospitality, like the rest of the visitor-friendly staff in their fashionably cut black lounge suits.)

The stunningly new, cosmo-casual restaurant just off Lake Calhoun occupies the longtime site of Nora's, and that's no accident. Tryg is the son of Nora Truelson, who, for decades, ran her popular hangout as a close cousin of a small-town diner. The days of red Naugahyde booths and hot turkey dinners ended as her senior clientele opted to spend its winters in Arizona. Capturing a younger, professional crowd who view dining as an evening's entertainment, the David Shea–designed new digs celebrate a natural, earthy look with banks of fieldstone, lots of glass to bring the outdoors in, and tabletops in warm wood tones under a high, barrel-vaulted ceiling of burnished copper. A roaring fire in the foyer smites winter's wind chill, while come summertime the outdoor seating captures the lake's breezes.

General Manager Lorenzo Cherubini (formerly of Giorgio's and Bakery on Grand) leads the front of the house, while Philip Dorwart, best known as the creative chef of the now-shuttered Table of Contents, heads the crew in the open kitchen. The menu he's assembled balances the fine line between the familiar and the innovative, all based on as much local fare as he can get his hands on. Appetizers, for instance, include a well-presented Bibb salad dressed with grilled pears, spiced pecans, and a buttermilk-herb vinaigrette or broiled oysters topped with bits of foie gras and shiitake mushrooms under a drizzle of sherry mignonette. The bar menu's apps are just as familiar, yet creative, such as devilled eggs dressed up with truffle oil and calamari dusted in panko crumbs for dipping in a lucque olive aioli.

Entrées prove to be hearty fare, starting with a simple-sounding meatloaf sandwich. But the meat is veal, served on pretzel bread with kalamata olive catsup and sweet potato shoestrings. Philip's chicken is rubbed with cinnamon before its stint on the rotisserie, then sided with hominy fries and roasted-pepper pan gravy. Diver scallops, as big as powder puffs, are sent out atop Parmesan risotto mingling with succulent shreds of braised oxtail under a topknot of crispy parsnip tendrils. An orange-lacquered duck also receives the benefit of the rotisserie, and the prime rib, served with bacon-mustard twice-baked potatoes, carries the scent of applewood. Vegetarians rate a blue-plate special of their own.

Son Cowles, wearing the toque of pastry chef, likewise reinvents familiar items such as apple cake and cherry tart in stylish presentations. The menu is backed by a solid wine list that spurns the knee-jerk labels in favor of affordable global finds.

YUMMY

2450 Nicollet Avenue, Minneapolis
(612) 870-8000 • yummyeat.com
$–$$; P; F

THE NAME IS APT, if not particularly Asian. Yummy—spelled out in a modern, meandering skein of neon atop a sprawling Eat Street building—introduced the Twin Cities to its unique culinary offerings in 2003. It answers a previously unserved need, catering both to the area's Chinese community, nostalgic for the tastes of home, and born-and-bred Minnesotans who crave un-airbrushed authenticity. The autos clogging its vast parking lot attest to the success of its mission.

Inside, the bland, beige setting houses booths along the windows and tables set for twosomes (a frustrating idea, however, here where sharing a multitude of dishes adds to the adventure) to dozens; they're often occupied by exuberant Asian families spinning the lazy Susan to deftly seize succulent morsels with chopsticks. Occasional nights of Asian karaoke when a wedding celebration is in progress can add to the noise level or feeling of participation, depending on one's mindset. Another wall has become a veritable aquarium, stacked with tanks of live seafood enjoying a last swim before being plucked to satisfy a diner's whim. Sea bass and lobsters, sure, but also eels, snails, sea urchins, and beyond figure on the extensive menu, swathed with sauces from the homeland.

Appetizers range from typical fare, such as egg rolls, chicken wings, and dumplings, to more elite preparations like crispy squab and quail with salt and hot pepper or the serious gourmand's jellyfish with pork knuckles and fried cuttlefish balls. Congee, the rice porridge that can prove so addictive, here allows many choices of additions, from frog legs, seafood, or chicken to preserved egg or dried scallops.

Barbecued meats are winners in this kitchen, and the options are many, from roast baby pig to duck, chicken, and spare ribs. Or choose those meats placed over rice or noodles. Fried rice takes on new flavors at Yummy when melded, for instance, with chicken and salted fish or prawns and poultry.

Noodles offer perennial comfort as a base for soups such as the beef brisket or fish ball numbers or the popular seafood and vegetable combination. Noodles also shine in dishes like dried scallop with black mushrooms or sautéed crab, lobster, mushrooms, or a "three sliced meat" combo. Conch with yellow chives and pan-fried noodles vies with beef chow fun in black bean sauce, while a tasty traditional Singapore rice noodle dish gets competition from Malaysian noodles, served spicy-hot.

The restaurant's young managers are as hip as heroes in a Hong Kong movie, and the platoon of servers is free with advice on what (and how much) to order. Try the eggplant hot pot, they'll tell you, and it's in your interest to listen up.

CHAPTER FOUR

South Minneapolis
and the Western Suburbs

AL VENTO

5001 34th Avenue South, Minneapolis
(612) 724-3009 • alventorestaurant.com
$$; O

IN OUR PARENTS' DAY, a politician's campaign promise used to be "a chicken in every pot." Let's update that for today's dining requirements and instead demand an Italian trattoria in every neighborhood.

Rising to the cause (and from the shadows of the former Marimar Café), al Vento brings homey Italian fare (and then some) to the underserved Lake Harriet neighborhood in south Minneapolis. The cozy corner storefront has been painted in colors of cappuccino and umber that warm the atmosphere. More love than money fed the transformation, which now flaunts villa-style "flagstone" flooring, sculpted hankies swathing the hanging lights, and a wagonwheel chandelier studded with red candles. The tiny bar and its half-dozen stools still stand ready for duty in the rear, below a swell collection of lesser-known labels of Italian wine. They're offered at prices quick to make loyalists of the couples and foursomes who haven't taken long to make their way here since the winds of fortune blew al Vento their way in autumn 2004.

Pane Vino Dolce was the training post of chef-owner John Hunt, and he's kept to its proven formula—antipasti, pizza, pasta, secondi, and sweets—with one or two tweaks seldom found in Rome (succulent, meaty crab cakes with dual aioli sauces, for instance). In classic Italian style, everything is made in-house, from the hearty peasant bread to dip in olive oil to the squeaky balls of mozzarella that star in the Caprese salad.

Start with a sampler of bruschetta, if you choose, or work your way through a list of antipasti that spotlights tomato bread soup enriched with Parmesan and basil, mussels steamed in saffron, a pair of scallops served with pomegranate seeds and fennel, and a couple of salads. The Caesar's a proven winner, and the plate of endive, roasted pears, Gorgonzola, and pancetta proves almost a meal in itself.

The kitchen's quartet of thin-crust pizzas includes a classic Neapolitan as well as a vegetarian pie loaded with red potatoes, spinach, and creamy Gorgonzola. John's five plates of pasta follow a similar trail, from ravioli rich with roasted pumpkin lapped in a brown butter/sage sauce, thick papardelle noodles tossed with a pork loin ragu and tomatoes, on to cannelloni, vegetarian-style.

The sextet of main dishes is just as brief and just as tempting, led by a lamb shank larger than decorum should permit, a Dijon-rosemary pork tenderloin sweetened with an orange reduction, and swordfish in the company of spinach risotto and tomato.

Servers—informed and friendly in equal measure—can steer you to the finales, too. Tiramisu, crème brûlée, and a chocolate tart: nothing startling, simply a trio of proven winners. Add a sweet sip of vin santo if you wish to gild the lily.

BAKERY ON GRAND

3804 Grand Avenue, Minneapolis
(612) 822-8260
$$

IT'S MORE THAN A BAKERY. And it certainly is grand. The cozy little café that opened in 2003 doubled its seating space (still scant) less than a year later—a sign of how eagerly the venture has been embraced by south Minneapolis locals, who've adopted it as "their" café.

It's not fancy—not a pretentious bone in the stockpot—but it's far from makeshift, too. Heavy, bare oak tables and straight-backed chairs occupy the similarly bare wood floor. Walls are unclad also, save for an arresting blue ribbon painted larger than life on one white surface. Old-fashioned, small-paned windows invite the morning sunlight to cheer the Bakery's breakfast brigade,

D'AMICO & SONS

3948 West 50th Street • Edina • (952) 926-1187
Multiple metro locations • damicoandsons.com

D'Amico Cucina, the company's flagship fine-dining restaurant, is a special-occasion destination. But for everyday—even twice a day—Cal/Italian fare with the same emphasis on quality and inventiveness, the 11 metrowide D'Amico & Sons dine in/carryout establishments are reason enough to sell your stove.

Here's the drill. Order at the counter from an extensive blackboard menu of pizzas, pastas, salads, and sandwiches plus a couple of entrées and pastries; then find yourself a table in the upbeat, softly stylish setting and await your order to be delivered. Kids' menus, office deliveries, and artisan breads to go are more pluses.

while at night votive candles glow among the shadows. The main room incorporates a working bakery counter crammed with beguiling treats to go, and it's possible to glimpse the kitchen crew at work behind the counter.

And work they do. The amazing level of talent has driven the place to many a foodie's top ten list. The front of the house is overseen by owners Doug and Jessica Anderson, who pulled the amazing group together. Together they make folks feel like family.

The chef is of consummate talent—and also has a knack for keeping things simple. Fewer than ten starters lead the seasonally changing menu, ranging from lobster bisque with tarragon-ricotta dumplings and a green salad dotted with port-Stilton toasts, to gravlax and terrines prepared by the kitchen's right-hand man. Fancier apps include a chanterelle risotto cake crisped in chive oil and a peppered apricot tartlet laden with juniper-scented foie gras. Of course, the meal begins with an assortment of the textured breads that are for sale as well.

Heavy white "diner" china sets off the seven entrées the chef has created for the week. Maybe it's a partnering of sea bass with parsnips, Swiss chard, and onion confit, or sea scallops with potato-shallot cakes and husky mustard greens laced with a truffle-watercress brown butter. Coq au vin, beef bourguignon, blanquette de veau, and other bistro staples take their turns on the menu, amid game offerings such as smoked baby pheasant served with sweet potato hash, brussels sprouts, and an apple cider and foie gras sauce or loin of venison with a chestnut-brioche charlotte drizzled with a cranberry and blood orange coulis for taste and color. Vegetarian plates are just as rustic and full of earthy flavors.

Desserts are bakery-simple rather than towers of spun sugar. The Bakery has become famous for its homemade butterscotch pudding, but the creamy panna cotta and lemon upside-down cake are just as appealing. So is the wine list, as grounded as the menu. And the breakfast brew's not bad, either.

BRODERS' PASTA BAR

5000 Penn Avenue South, Minneapolis
(612) 925-9202 • broders.com
$$; F; P; no reservations

YEARS BACK, this was once a gas station, but these days the folks of south Minneapolis fill up on its casual, modern Italian fare, pumped out by station attendants in their chefs' whites. High-octane red sauce and easy-on-the-chassis antipasti are among the house specialties. And if someone asks, "Check your oil?" it's the bottle of extra-virgin on the white-clad table they're referring to.

BRODERS' CUCINA ITALIANA

2308 West 50th Street • Minneapolis • (612) 925-3113
www.broders.com

Inspired by a love for all things Italian, back in 1982 Tom and Molly Broder decided to share their passion with the rest of the city's purists of taste. Their gourmet specialty shop and deli has educated many a Minneapolitan on what fresh mozzarella tastes like as well as on the value of top-quality olive oil and balsamic vinegar to dress a salad. Those imported items are part of hundreds on offer, including cheeses and sausages, dried pasta, olives, and chocolates from the Old Country. They're supplemented by items made in-house to enjoy here at the shop's handful of tables, to take home, or to have delivered. House-made sauces, pizzas, pans of lasagna, and threateningly decadent desserts ease the tremors of party-giving and provide instant pleasure around the kitchen table. The Broders also operate Broders' Pasta Bar across the street (see below).

Sure, cars can still park in the concrete arena in front of the café, but Molly Broder, aided by her husband, Tom, has created a stone wall as a buffer to insulate parking from the inviting patio lined with greenery and comfy benches, à la Tuscany, that face the "villa" of white brick and windows wearing tall shutters clad in green.

Inside, the atmosphere is contemporary and relaxed in equal measure. Walls washed in the warm tones of café latte hold posters with modern Italian flair. Within, the windows are shuttered, too, conspiring with the soft mood lighting to create a cozy cocoon for dining. Families and parties of neighbors seek tables lining the perimeter, while singles and young couples on the run choose a stool at the central counter square, the better to catch the action in the open kitchen just beyond.

The restaurant's antipasti are designed for sharing. Consider a plate of Italian sausage sequined with red grapes, roasted sweet red peppers, and a splash of balsamic reduction. Or try mussels in your choice of red or white sauce or perhaps the crostini or zuppa of the day, and make sure to glance at the evening's appetizer pizza selection.

Three salad offerings segue to the next course: a toss of greens with pine nuts and Parmesan, a classic Caesar, and a Greek salad borrowed from across the Aegean. Among the pasta and risotto offerings, it's hard to resist the ravioli di zucca—squash-filled pasta swimming in brown butter, sage, and cheese. The Broders also knows how to perform the simple classics, including penne with rosemary, cream, and tomato; tagliatelle Bolognese, a rich meat sauce; and lasagna—not so simple here, with its cameo appearance of red crab.

Signature specialties include fettucine with chicken, wild mushrooms, and pine nuts as well as an unusual marriage of sea bass, kalamata olives, and cherry tomatoes tossed with spaghetti noodles. Risotto lovers delight in the combo of that aristocratic rice with slipper lobster, cranberry beans, roasted red peppers, and fresh basil.

Dolce? For sure. Sweets range from crisp biscotti to dip into your espresso to substantial undertakings such as the Bestia Nera (Black Devil) flourless chocolate cake that earns its moniker; supple cheesecakes; and an elegant caramel custard. Wines are Italian, of course, offered along with imported designer waters.

CAFÉ 28

2724 West 43rd Street, Minneapolis
(612) 926-2800 • cafetwentyeight.com
$-$$; F; O

NO THREE-ALARM CHILI, but the Mexican broth, humming with adobo chilies, comes close. It's almost worth coming down with the flu so someone could bring you a bowl. And it's typical of the seasonally changing menu of Café 28, at home in a former firehouse in Linden Hills. These days the fire is in the belly of owner Linda Hoag, a longtime wine rep and Linden Hills resident, who took up with the idea that her neighbors deserved a café they could walk to (as she herself walks to work)—a home away from the homes for her professional clientele, with their virtually unused kitchens, where microwave meals eaten standing over the sink leave a lot to be desired.

Because their tastes outpace their cooking skills, she felt she had something to offer her neighbors: food that is cooked from scratch, "not terribly fancy, made with good ingredients." She's made a go of it with low overhead but sky-high ambitions that fire (pardon) a modest but creative menu.

That's the key to the success of her comely little bistro, dotted with tables where once the fire trucks stood ready to roar away on signal. These days a many-paned French door fills the space from which the trucks once sped; it opens to a pocket-sized patio for outdoor eating in the summer months. In wintertime, the former station makes a cozy place to hunker down for first-rate sustenance, amid walls the color of guacamole hung with works of local artists. And Haug herself can be found behind the cash register, where her roving eye makes sure that patrons leave well satisfied. Some bring their kids (there's a special menu); some amble in solo with the evening's paperwork; others hook up with friends after grazing the boutiques that line the intersection.

Slender-crusted pizzas almost buckle under their load of portobellos consorting with crumbles of pungent Gorgonzola upon a layer of caramelized onions, making it a nice way to start the evening. Or turn to a potage of curried cream of pumpkin, or the spicy chicken quesadilla.

Main courses such as an open-faced turkey sandwich (yes, with gravy, cranberries, and mashed potatoes) threaten to bring tears to the eyes of those yearning for the real food of the good old days. Haug's steak sandwich and cheeseburger (made with healthy bison meat) also revisit the classics, albeit with must-try updates like horseradish, blue cheese, and caramelized onions as accessories.

A buffalo flank steak, big as South Dakota, sings with a flurry of Latin spices, while a grouper makes its debut coated in cumin and pumpkin seeds. Pork tenderloin, chicken in several ethnic-inspired treatments, and meal-sized salads complete the manageable list. Desserts receive the same TLC in the kitchen. Again, they're of the homey persuasion, such as the apple crisp, served warm with ice cream.

The café's list of wine and beer is just as brief, and just as workable. Servers have been known to bring samples for the undecided before committing to a beverage—yet another of the friendly gestures that the neighbors repay with ardent loyalty.

CALIFORNIA CAFÉ

368 South Boulevard, Mall of America, Bloomington
(952) 854-2233 • californiacafe.com
$$; F; P

THE MALL OF AMERICA is awesome in anyone's book. Love it or loathe it, the biggest retail venue in the country earns that adjective big-time. But the moment comes when even a marathon shopper yearns for a break.

There's the fast food court, a couple of chain concepts on the main floor—and then there's the California Café. Located on the third level, this cheery, upbeat setting, comfy enough to accommodate Champs Sports shoppers yet with enough sophistication to please the Nordstrom's devotee, is dressed in California mode—all white and bright, with breezy accents in swipes of crayon colors. An open kitchen in the rear takes justified pride in its San Francisco–style pizzas and healthy, meal-sized salads suited to starlets in LA.

Those who cannot get their fill of dining-as-theater head for the balcony. It overlooks the amusement-park attractions of Camp Snoopy, so expect the screams of roller coaster riders to punctuate your meal with predictable frequency. Kids love it; lovers don't—and move to a booth within.

In both venues, the café's cadre of alert and well-trained servers are prompt to recite the specials of the day in addition to a menu that pays homage to our Land O' Lakes as well as the sunny West Coast. Thus, you'll find a smoked chicken and wild rice soup among a list of starters that also salutes a plate of California cheeses, served with roasted garlic and crostini painted with melted Cambazola and tomato chutney.

The list of starters also spotlights winsome salads like the handsome plate of prosciutto-wrapped peaches atop butter lettuce, joined by candied walnuts and California blue cheese. Or start with soy-glazed tuna lollipops brightened with watermelon salsa; a blue crab cake dressed with lemon-caper aioli; or Mongolian lamb chops resting on mint slaw.

Again the dual Minnesota-California roots take hold among the seafood entrées. Choose an Alaskan halibut with blue-corn hush puppies, avocado salad, and corn salsa or a Minnesota walleye dressed for the mall with artichoke wontons and dill tartar sauce. Meat eaters gravitate to the rack of lamb embellished with an eggplant lasagna roll, baby green beans, and garlic jus—if they haven't succumbed to the grilled New York strip nesting on white cheddar mashed potatoes, that is. And oh, those pizzas! Anyone for the house-smoked salmon number?

Flights of wine augment the genteel list, while margaritas, sangria, and mojitos also answer well as shoppers' therapy.

CONVENTION GRILL

3912 Sunnyside Road, Edina
(952) 920-6881
$–$$; F; P; no alcohol

WELCOME TO THE quintessential greasy spoon. The Convention Grill was established in 1934, and some swear the career waitresses in their white uniforms have hoisted those trays since the very beginning. The setting hasn't inched forward during those decades, either, simply added another layer of grease to the tiles as generation after generation files through the door for their fix of diner food. Best seats in the house are the counter stools in front of the fry cooks as they ricochet between flipping those hand-pattied burgers and performing magic with spuds and onion rings. Dog-eared placards above their station announce what's also good, and always has been: root beer floats and hot fudge sundaes.

Patrons in the nearby booths and banquettes of vintage oxblood leatherette can enjoy that short-order floorshow, too, while those in the second room beyond, boasting sunnier and more spacious seating, are spared a bit of the splatter and patter but also sacrifice a slice of retro ambience. That larger room, with mirror tiles above the tables, ceiling fans, and linoleum squares paving the floor, sports an almost Aztec pattern in its determinedly cheery color scheme of pink and turquoise. Still, the booths are bigger, and the room shortens an otherwise-endless wait on a Saturday—prime time for families hauling minivans of suburban kids or granddad initiating the younger generation to the grand old era. There's even a juke box (remember those?).

This is not the place to skimp on calories. Portions are enormous, and you can smell them coming from the parking lot. The hallowed, all-American dietary trio is the way to go here: hamburger, fries, and a chocolate malt (delivered with seconds in a silvery canister). Yet the homemade chicken soup (refills readily sold here, too) and the meatloaf sandwich boast a devoted corps of fans as well, as does the husky grilled-cheese sandwich. That's half the menu, right there.

The other page is devoted to old-fashioned soda fountain fare. Malts come in 16 flavors and two sizes. The choice of sundaes is nearly as vast, but the homemade hot fudge number is far and away the winner; add bananas for no extra charge. Floats and phosphates also find their loyal following. No liquor is sold, but who needs it with these old-time enticements?

CORNER TABLE

4257 Nicollet Avenue South, Minneapolis
(612) 823-0011 • cornertablerestaurant.com
$$; reservations only for six or more

SCOTT PAMPUCH has found the answer. Two restaurants failed in the spot he now occupies, a pizzeria and the former NE Thyme, where he served as chef. As chef-owner this round, he's made some small and seemingly simple changes that add up to success. The tiny corner space (thus the name) in a south Minneapolis neighborhood is not much bigger than your dining room at home and always seemed—and was—cramped, loud, and, well, garish.

Somehow Pampuch has maneuvered a more comfortable layout. He's also opened up the front window to view and done wonders with mirrors on his walls of muted greens and browns. Comfy chairs and simple table settings add to the casually sophisticated aura, abetted by romantic lighting. And yes, you can still spot the chef at work on the range through the open "window" behind the tiny bar.

His appealing, diverse menu changes monthly, depending on what part of the culinary world has caught his fancy lately—maybe Caribbean, maybe Italian, most likely regional Midwestern, too. Starters—some hot, some cold—may include a splendid salad of roasted beets and cashews in sesame oil or ravioli plumped with a puree of parsnips, served in a faint green sauce of parsley juice stirred with crème fraiche. In season, a classic Caprese salad comes to life with ripe heirloom tomatoes, squeaky-fresh mozzarella, and basil straight from the garden.

Beef, lamb, and game are always solid choices here, as is the free-range organic chicken, simply rubbed with herbs and sauced with a sensuous meld of honey and smoked tomatoes. Roast duck, moistened with a sweet-tart berry sauce, nests on a pillow of wild rice. Perfectly cooked pork loin rates a side of root-vegetable gratin, which comes near to stealing the show. Vegetarians flock here for Pampuch's creative pastas and risotto dishes, as well as a cassoulet composed of a myriad of beans and tasty grains.

It's nice—and rather rare—to find a cheese sampler in a local restaurant. The Corner Table's selections salute Midwestern products as a tasty dessert in itself or prelude to a sweet. Four finales are offered nightly, including a chocolate trio highlighted by a black-as-midnight molten chocolate cake. Bread pudding, studded with apples and walnuts in a splash of brandy, gains oomph from a stellar roasted-carrot sorbet. Or choose crepes, filled with persimmons and candied ginger in a honey sauce. The café also offers a four-course tasting menu of surprises, giving the chef a chance to play in the kitchen and wow his trusting guests. Wine from the well-chosen, value-rich list is served in classy Riedel tumblers.

The Corner Table draws more than its share of neighborhood couples for its weekend breakfasts who'd rather read the news than cook, and who can blame them? It's truly breakfast fare—no pastas, no salmon, no crème brûlée. Instead, you'll find scrambled eggs with chives and mushrooms, a classic steak-and-eggs with a side of cottage fries, stoneground oatmeal swimming in cream, French toast, maybe a frittata. And lots of good, strong coffee to keep the conversations humming.

THE CRAFTSMAN

4300 East Lake Street, Minneapolis
(612) 722-0175 • craftsmanrestaurant.com
$$

THERE GOES THE NEIGHBORHOOD. South Minneapolis is peppered with Arts and Crafts bungalows—simple, clean-cut, matter-of-fact homes of the working class when they were built. Today, they're prized by a new generation of first-time homeowners, who prefer their compactness and community over a five-bedroom castle in the burbs. At the tail end of 2004, The Craftsman opened to serve these new residents, as well as a wider congregation of diners attracted by another bright example of the growing chef/patron movement that celebrates a desire to cook honest, mildly inventive, and incredibly appealing food for friends and neighbors.

Chef Mike Phillips is just such a believer. As former chef/owner fo the shuttered Chet's Taverna, his finesse behind the range was sorely missed till he found a new home in this former burger-pizza stop, modestly refurbished in homage to the environs' Prairie heritage. Wood warms the bare floors, tables are flanked with straight-backed chairs, and walls are accented with green, russet, and butter yellow and hung with Crafts-style "stained glass" sconces and schoolhouse lights.

The craftsman in the owner seems to apply to the man behind the stove, too—no highfalutin' "artist" image, no inflated ego, simply an artisan's dedication to his work—in this case, producing bounteous plates of interesting fare on a menu that changes monthly. Start with a carrot-orange soup livened with a perky ginger cream, perhaps, or a refreshing salad of arugula and mint strewn with pears and pungent blue cheese. Or PEI mussels steamed in local Summit brewery's hearty oatmeal stout. Continue with organic chicken served with a purple potato terrine and braised Belgian endive or salmon paired with roasted shiitake mushrooms aside a Southern-inspired collage of spicy pork-fried green beans. Pork chops come with a three-apple stuffing aside husky leaves of chard and a fingerling potato and chorizo hash. Short ribs pick up a subtle Asian accent when braised in mirin and served with daikon and an orange salad. Vegetarians delight in the kitchen's substantial risotto, tossed with squash, green spangles of rapini, toasted pepita seeds, and a citrus molasses.

The dessert list would be right at home in those bungalows' Arts and Crafts kitchens, too. Case in point: banana bread pudding mined with roasted walnuts under a mocha sauce or cranberry crisp topped with lemon-buttermilk ice cream.

The Craftsman's wine list consciously salutes all-American vintners, primarily lesser-known finds from the West Coast. There's a nice offering of half bottles, too. Servers haven't a haughty air among them. Although they're as casual as the homey surroundings, underneath that laid-back attitude lies a wealth of information on menu prep, wine nuances, and the state of the bike path along the nearby Mississippi River.

KINCAID'S

8400 Normandale Lake Boulevard, Bloomington
(952) 921-2255

380 Saint Peter Street, Saint Paul
(651) 602-9000 • kincaids.com
$$–$$$

KINCAID'S CAME OUR WAY from a restaurant group in the Pacific Northwest during the late 80s, settling on a Bloomington office complex for its first location. The angled windows of the tower it anchors frame a picturesque pocket of a woodland park, complete with marshy pond. The indoor space, dressed in dark wood and forest green, reflects this affinity to nature. The manly setting, accented by lots of gleaming brass and prints of hunting and fishing scenes, conveys a clubhouse atmosphere, with tables in alcoves and against dividers to accommodate the private business discussions that dominate the lunch trade as well as celebratory dinners, both romantic and financial.

A second location opened in 2000 in downtown Saint Paul to answer the plea of "What's to eat?" before or after an event or concert. It's a little breezier and brighter in its décor. Both sites offer lighter menus in their comfy cocktail lounges and a similar basic philosophy behind the kitchen door. It's this: Kincaid's is a fish, chop, and steakhouse, plain and simple. Prime quality is foremost and showcased in the center of the plate. Accompaniments are always interesting and well thought out but not designed to steal the show.

A fresh sheet details which fish have been flown in that very morning. King of that list is Kincaid's King salmon, when it's available. Aficionados make their reservation just as soon as they hear it's arrived. Shellfish win pride of place, too, leading off with chili-rubbed smoked shrimp served with a side of barbecue hollandaise, mashed potatoes, and smoked and roasted vegetables. The kitchen's plump crab cakes often come with a sweet-and-sour sauce, while sea scallops, skewered with rosemary and pan-seared, may be dressed with a compote of sour cherries and figs.

Kincaid's stakes its reputation just as solidly on its prime ribs of beef, slow-roasted on rock salt after almost a month of dry-aging. The tender New York cut is a close second, while applewood-smoked pork loin, rubbed with molasses, coriander seeds, and black pepper, vies with rosemary-crusted lamb sirloin in a dijon-garlic marinade for top billing, too. Good news for the undecided: Several of Kincaid's versions of surf and turf make choosing a bit easier.

That's also the ticket with the appetizer sampler platter, offering a trio of the kitchen's most popular starters, including smoked shrimp, char-siu pork lollipops, and the house signature, hot Dungeness crab dip, served with the addictive rosemary pan bread that accompanies each meal.

Clam chowder, New England–style, and any salad dressed with the restaurants' own Maytag blue cheese recipe are other top choices, especially at lunchtime, when they contribute to the soup-salad-sandwich combinations (choose two out of three).

Servers are star grads of the company's intensive training drill; they take guests' needs (and whims) most seriously, and with a smile.

LA FOUGASSE

Hotel Sofitel, 5601 West 78th Street, Bloomington
(612) 835-1900
$$; P; O

IT'S HARDER TO PRONOUNCE than to enjoy. This smart-casual restaurant, launched a few seasons back as the new flagship dining concept of Hotel Sofitel, was named for a special French pretzel-twisted bread, enriched with herbs and olive oil

The chic café has reinstated the Bloomington Hotel as a home for destination dining. Half the fun is ooh-la-la-ing the café's fantasyland setting, which is like Alice's Wonderland for grownups—a whimsy splashed with sunny Provençal tones of azure and butter-yellow. Golden sheers, backed by cherry-red portieres, shade the floor-to-ceiling windows, beyond which are outdoor tables that welcome summer diners. Indoors, chairs upholstered in rich tones of gold and cherry boast cheeky mix-and-match patterns. Walls painted in Provençal sky blue hold golden-toned niches showcasing blown-glass art. The open kitchen and bar preceding the display sport hand-tiled accents; two-sided fireplaces serve as room dividers, as do high-backed benches in the same spirited designs.

FRANCE 44

4351 France Avenue South • Minneapolis • (612) 925-3252
www.france44.com

The address is in south Minneapolis, but the setting is straight out of wine country—a lofty ceiling with rafters of raw timber and unusually spacious aisles in the state-of-the-art wine shop, marked with "road signs" directing customers to the Loire, Burgundy, Alsace, and the like. An entry display entices those on budgets slimmer than their palates with a special shelf of bottles: "18 for $18."

The user-friendly deli sports equally sunny and attractive quarters lined with shelves of classy condiments. Refrigerator cases burst with cheeses, sausages, pâtés, and cured fish, augmented by an eat-in/takeout menu that makes mealtime easy. Soups like Grandma's cabbage or corn-crab bisque come with baguettes and, if you like, a salad or a sandwich (pecan chicken, meatball Parmigiano, muffuletta, and a dozen more). And the chocolate truffles are worth penance in dietary purgatory.

France 44 also offers dinners for two on selected weeknights; the set price includes salad, bread, and a bottle of wine.

Plates are rimmed in blue and yellow, too, to complement the kitchen's Provençal flair. A good plan is to start with one of two "tasting trees," layered with a half-dozen appetizers to share, including crispy ravioli of scallops and zucchini; frog legs in a pesto marinade; a chorizo and shrimp tartine; and Gorgonzola flan. Soups include a Mediterranean rendering of French onion soup, served here with a creamy black-olive tapenade, and a rich fish soup (think bouillabaisse) dressed up with croutons, Parmesan, and a spicy rouille sauce.

Fish takes center stage on the list of entrées, highlighted by potato-crusted yellowfin tuna with an eggplant napoleon, or loup de mer set on saffron pearl-pasta risotto, plus a full-fledged bouillabaisse Marseillaise in traditional style. Or venture to the lamb, served with an onion confit tart and potato gnocchi, or duck accented by porcini mushrooms and, mais oui, escargot. And, of course, that crusty twist of fougasse is there to sop up the tasty juices.

French pastries follow, and they're the same quality as in the takeout counter set out to ambush your taste buds as you leave.

The wine list heralds scores of French labels, and servers, speaking with the sweet accents of their native land, do them justice. Fellow guests range from the visiting Francophiles who gravitate to this hotel to their local counterparts, eager to try out their language lessons, alongside groups of friends and family and romantic duos, who linger at those window tables to savor a final sip of wine.

LEVAIN

4762 Chicago Avenue South, Minneapolis
(612) 823-7111 • restaurantlevain.com
$$$; P; reservations suggested

ONE PEEK AT LEVAIN and befuddled travelers might be excused for thinking they were in San Francisco. But no, it's south Minneapolis—and a formerly underserved part of it, at that—that lays claim to one of the hottest dining rooms east of the Bay. The modest storefront boasts no bold marquee, not even much of a sign on the door as a giveaway that it's the place to see, be seen, and eat like a spoiled San Franciscan while craning and posing. (Do reserve, and count yourself lucky if the somewhat aloof phone messenger calls back to say you're in.)

The room is almost monastically simple: a bare wooden floor and creamy walls with heavy iron lighting fixtures are the only accents. Tables are stripped to bare essentials, too: crisp, white expanses of linen unburdened by bud vases or candles. Severe, unpadded chairs contribute little in the way of comfort.

The source of comfort lies in the kitchen, open along one side to capture the chefs' dance line as they sweep along their stations. These days Steven Brown (formerly of Loring, the Local, and Rock Star) pulls the team together, and he does it so well. He sends out an *amuse* as a welcome, along with what's arguably the best bread in town—a mix-and-match basket from the ovens of Turtle Bakery, the sister property around the corner.

The starter list is limited to seven items, but that doesn't mean choosing is easy. Levain's house salad is dressed in sherry caramel and topped with anise-tomato conserves and whipped brie. Soft clouds of polenta rest under a few leaves of spinach, chunks of chicken, mushrooms, and bits of buffalo mozzarella. Or summon a petite quail, which arrives with a retinue of crispy sweetbreads bathed in balsamic brown butter and sprinkled with pineapple sage.

KHANH TRAN

Pastry Chef, Levain

While male chefs traditionally man the stockpot, it's often women who rule the rolling pin. Levain's pastry chef, Khanh Tran, absorbed her love of sweet finales while growing up in a family that launched the cities' first upscale Vietnamese restaurant, Matin. Motivated to perfect her pastry skills, she enrolled in the famed Culinary Institute of America and, upon graduation, honed her talents in the San Francisco kitchen of China Moon. Encouraged by its owner, the legendary Barbara Tropp, she set off to study in France at Ritz Escoffier. "In France, the work ethic was so great; everyone was so passionate about food. It was a man's world, a European world, and I barely knew kitchen French. But you keep your eyes open, use common sense, and balance where you are and where you're going." At Levain, "I try to cook for myself and put love into it." Her personal favorites: "Anything chocolate, and warm. And I like the tartness of fruit."

Amid the seven entrées is a vegetarian ovation, such as roasted beets, cippolini onions, grains of faro, and Gorgonzola dolce. Steve's version of surf and turf is a New York strip sided with blue prawns, served with asparagus, fava beans, sweet corn, and pimientos. But fish is where he really shines, as proven in numbers like halibut atop grilled fennel with countneck clams and coriander sage, or king salmon in a sweet apricot soup afloat with snap peas and shards of prosciutto.

A cheese plate makes a nice dessert offering, but with Levain's venerated pastry chef behind the counter, who can be blamed for succumbing to temptations like caramel in three visions: crème caramel, caramel chocolate tart, and burnt-caramel ice cream? A buttermilk cream custard brightened with strawberries and rhubarb jam makes fine eating, too. And as the bill arrives, so does a plate of madeleines to nibble.

The wine list celebrates smaller vineyards; count on Levain's attentive staff for recommendations. Five- and seven-course tasting menus are available to ease problems with decision-making.

111

LORD FLETCHER'S

3746 Sunset Drive, Spring Park
(952) 471-8513 • lordfletchers.com
$$–$$$; P; O

HERE IN THE LAND of 10,000 lakes, dining on the shoreline of one of those belles of the landscape ranks at the top of the chart as a way to celebrate our Minnesota summer. Lord Fletcher's, anchoring prime shoreline on Lake Minnetonka, has been reeling in repeat customers for decades, while also reeling in (from Canadian waters) enough walleye to keep them coming back for the menu's heralded specialty.

The main dining room wears its Olde English dress code well and provides most diners with a window view. The more informal pub on the lower level captures the boating crowd in their topsiders and dungarees, and the open-air deck fills rapidly with exurban sun worshipers enjoying a presunset libation or whiling away a sunny Saturday afternoon.

Wintertime brings its own set of visual rewards, with a view of a snowy lakescape straight from Currier and Ives. The dining room is especially charming when done up in a Dickensian way around the December holidays, when Fletcher's sterling silver prime rib cut tends to outsell even the legendary walleye.

Few devotees break with tradition and start with anything other than Fletcher's jumbo shrimp cocktail—unless it's to indulge in that legendary walleye in the form of lodge-style pan-fried cakes, served with red cabbage slaw and a honey mustard remoulade. The house salad is a must as well—a bowl of mixed greens topped with sunflower seeds, Parmesan cheese, and a creamy peppercorn dressing. Those who feel the urge to start a tradition of their own opt for the Mediterranean-style moons of mozzarella topping vine-ripened tomatoes in pesto and balsamic vinegar—certainly a hit at the height of summer— or a classic Caesar, anchovies optional.

We've raved about the walleye—served with au gratin potatoes or saffron rice along with scampi butter and tartar sauce, of course—and the succulent prime rib. But the shrimp and scallops, dashed with a touch of caper butter and skewered on a sprig of rosemary, and the coconut-crusted tiger shrimp, anointed with Thai red curry sauce for added interest, are strong contenders, too. And if you've been boating all day and nothing but a steak will ease the sunburn, Fletcher's T-bone or rib eye will accommodate. To ease the pain of decision-making, Fletcher's offers several combo plates, each leading off with a six ounce sterling silver filet mignon. And there are plenty of suitable companions on the wine list with which to accent the evening.

LOUIS XIII

2670 Southdale Shopping Center, Edina
(952) 746-4938 • louisxiiirestaurant.com
$$$; P

THE CITIES' FANCIEST French restaurant—pronounced with your best French accent as "Louie Trez"—began its reign in May 2004. Why name it for this rather unremarkable French emperor? French-Algerian restaurant mogul David Fhima (Mpls Café, Fhima's), spiffy in his fresh chef's whites, merely smiles in answer. Well, perhaps it just wouldn't do to name it after Louis XIII's successor, the Sun King, because this is definitely a place that comes alive at night.

It inspires a bit of a double-take to encounter this glitzy dining palace smack in the middle of the Southdale Shopping Center—more Vegas than Versailles, starting with the façade, a repro of a classic French painting magnified about a million times.

Behind the high-energy bar rises the see-through, floor-to-ceiling wine racks that may prove a necessity as well as a promo option when a list contains 1,300 labels. A glass elevator steals yet another piece of showmanship from Vegas. At each side of the elevator, cocooned in gauzy netting, parade an arcade of kiss-

A BAKER'S WIFE'S PASTRY SHOP

4200 28th Avenue South • Minneapolis • (612) 729-6898

The cult is growing. These days, the neighborhood's foodies find they must share "their" corner bakery with citywide fans of good things from the oven. The tiny site on an unremarkable stretch of south Minneapolis is the source of superbly crafted baked goods that celebrate the heritage of our heartland's farmsteads. No croissants, no bagels. Instead, coffee cakes, tender cookies, sugared doughnuts, cinnamon rolls, and their caramel-pecan cousins are the Baker's Wife's forte, along with sturdy loaves and sandwich buns of all demeanor. Coffee is available for the impatient among us who feel the urge to grab a table amid the setting's clutter of tchotchkes and demolish the treats in the white paper bag post haste.

ing booths, large enough for a ménage a quatre, however. And if you're not occupied with smooching, you can view the jumbo glassed-in kitchen, bright and glossy as a surgical theater. A communal table gets a full frontal view.

Behind this working hub, the walls of a small dining room are dressed in an undulating curtain of midnight blue superintended by a comtempo beaded chandelier. On the lower level, similar red-draped rooms welcome private functions.

Fhima's menu hails the familiar French classics, but often with a twist. Pour Commencer, as the appetizer heading on the menu indicates, contains a listing of pâté, charcuterie, smoked salmon, and a frisee salad, to be sure, but pay attention. The mussels of a vintage bistro's list are paired with a lemongrass Gruyere pesto in this kitchen, and a traditional salade Niçoise is shifted a few degrees off-center with another Asian touch. They're works of art. So is the Caesar salad, sent out to wow crowds with its pair of Parmesan chopsticks.

Among the close to 20 main plates, you'll find others fused with Oriental flavors, such as a flaky fillet of cod coated in a tangerine-teriyaki glaze, or coq au vin reconstructed with bok choy and rice wine rather than the red stuff. Rack of lamb, dressed in sesame seeds, receives a teriyaki glaze, and pork chops appear in an apple-hoisin lacquer. The good news is, these fusion fancies work.

So do Fhima's straight-arrow French renditions, such as a pastry-wrapped beef tenderloin paired with Roquefort, steak au poivre in a Cognac-peppercorn sauce, and sole aside a suave lobster mousseline.

Desserts are more staid. Presented tableside from a roving cart, it's clear the pastry chef takes few chances, offering crème caramel, tiramisu, tarte tatin, berry tart, and the like. And, thank goodness, the platoons of hosts, sommeliers, and servers abandon authentic French aloofness for genial rounds of Minnesota nice.

MOJITO

4656 Excelsior Boulevard, Saint Louis Park
(952) 922-6656
$$; P

MOJITO, NAMED FOR a trendy Brazilian cocktail, debuted in May 2003 as the metro's first churrascuria, a concept as sizzling as that early summer evening. On the lookout for a second successful opportunity, the folks behind Bobino scooted down to Rio to experience the South American version of a steakhouse and see how the concept would fly back home in lefseland.

The answer is, just fine. We Minnesotans like our red meat. And our mojitos.

COASTAL SEAFOODS

2330 Minnehaha Avenue • Minneapolis • (612) 724-7425

74 Snelling Avenue • Saint Paul • (651) 698-4888

840 East Lake Street • Wayzata • (952) 249-3878

What? Fresh fish in flyover land? Well, thanks to the airport, you bet. Coastal Seafoods, which Suzanne Weinstein bravely launched in 1981 to bring fresh fish to Minnesota, carries upward of 50 varieties flown in on a daily basis, selling 50 tons a week to walk-in customers angling for tonight's dinner as well as to the area's premier restaurants. Manager Tim Lauer calls on 50 sources to net everything from salmon—the hands-down bestseller—to exotica like Ecuadorian tilapia, Hawaiian opah, Buckley Bay oysters, and, of course, live lobsters. Lauer also teaches how-to classes in seafood selection and preparation to neophytes. He's now got a cookbook on the market, too.

In the newly rejuvenated retail stretch of Excelsior Avenue in Saint Louis Park it takes its stand, with views of passing perambulators or, even better, the open kitchen to one side where that celebrated beef—and more—is grilled, and where they do their magic with those sassy sauces. The bar in the rear offers a few more shadows for romantic assignations, while under the cathedral ceiling, the banquettes and tables fill up with foursomes and even large family parties, eager to savor what it's all about.

Welcome to Brazil, and beyond. These days chef Pat Weber, who trained at the famed Culinary Institute of America, uses his talents to finesse what he calls "crossroads cuisine," a fusion of elements that wander beyond Brazil's borders. Think pizza and pasta with sunny flavors like a Calabrese crust loaded with sweet Italian sausage, or penne tossed with tomatoes, cream, garlic, and Argentinean cheese. Salads segue from a Tijuana Caesar to a classy toss of watercress with walnuts, apples, and Spanish cheese. But it's in the appetizer list that Pat's imagination really takes over. He stuffs his flaky empanada pastries with savory beef picadillo or mozzarella laced with herbs, then sends out a dipping sauce of smoky sweet red peppers, so tasty it should be patented. His Brazilian shrimp croquettes with a spicy aioli vie with his griddled Argentinean provolone for richness, while a Mexican posole—a soup-stew bursting with hominy and pork—proves the ultimate in comfort food.

But let's talk about the churrascuria. Spit-roasted meats lead off with top sirloin, followed by pork loin rubbed in sweet chiles under a honey glaze, leg of lamb, and free-range chicken. Viands where fire-grilling is the forte include four choices of beefsteaks as well as a combination platter of chorizo, longaniza, and calabrese sausages. Served à la carte, they invite side orders such as grilled vegetables, fried plantains, garlicky yucca, and more to the table.

Feijoada, the traditional stew that serves as Sunday brunch in Rio, appears as a chef's special wherein Pat incorporates side plates of smoked pork, sausage, collard greens, and a welcome touch of orange to the tureen, to be mixed in at will by each diner. A Brazilian shellfish stew enhanced with peppers and coconut leads the seafood list.

A grand way to experiment with this cuisine is to order family-style (minimum of four people) in a plan that allows one salad, three fire-roasted meats, and three side dishes for the table. Then, if there's even the mere possibility that dessert is on your mind, consider the sweet empanadas painted with a drizzle of guava and a chile-chocolate ribbon.

Half of the wine list is devoted to labels from south of the equator. Servers know their way around the menu, so when in doubt, trust their taste buds.

NAPA VALLEY GRILLE

Mall of America, Bloomington
(952) 858-9934 • calcafe.com
$$–$$$; P

DESTINATION DINING in a mall—especially the Mall of America, the largest mall known to man (and certainly woman)? It's not an oxymoron if you're speaking of the Napa Valley Grille. The clubby, masculine setting, full of moody shadows and lots of dark wood, attracts its share of tourists, that's a given. But it also a does a robust business in corporate entertaining as well as serving knowing local couples. They're all on the prowl for food with flair and vintages to match, gleaned from the café's award-winning wine list, which celebrates the vineyards of its California valley namesake and does them proud in the extensive offerings. The Grille hosts periodic wine dinners at which those visiting vintners often are on hand to strut their stuff.

Executives with their briefcases aside, the Grille is also delighted to soothe weary shoppers with its extensive menu of comfort food kicked up a notch.

And, as one of the mall's original tenants over a decade ago, it's stood the test of time.

These days chef Royal Dahlstrom, the former toque behind the stove at the now-shuttered La Toscana, heads the kitchen brigade. His forte here is trading on the staples of the Grille's West Coast heritage, yet grounding that California trendiness in good old Minnesota common sense.

Starters highlight a roasted tomato soup, deep with flavor and accented with horseradish cream. Or choose a sampler of Wine Country cheese, served with roasted onions and citrus-fig chutney. Prosciutto-roasted nectarines paired with blue cheese and basil cream demonstrate that the chef is inventive but not over the top.

You have to wonder about his, er, original West-meets-Midwest Caesar, however—romaine dressed in a garlic-smoked lake trout dressing—until a forkful proves he's not so crazy after all. Or stick with a salad of spinach nesting a round of baked goat cheese under a shower of walnuts.

Roasted pork tenderloin with a barbecue rub turns Minnesotan with wild rice and a sweet-corn broth, while wild fennel with pollen-seared halibut, served with heirloom tomatoes, comes straight out of San Francisco. And where the cumin-seared ostrich came from, who knows? But with the poblano polenta at its side and a dollop of salsa verde, it captures diners' attention and delight. Duck three ways is the answer for those who want it all: confit, smoked breast, and pâté, with a cherry sauce to boot. But the truly undecided palate may appreciate the chef's Trio Off the Grill, composed of tenderloins of beef and pork and a petite lamb T-bone, served with grilled asparagus and a smoked pepper vinaigrette. Not exactly finger food for the Ladies Who Lunch, you say? Quite true. But the Grille does offer ladies-only wine nights and other special events for businesswomen armed with healthy palates.

PANE VINO DOLCE

819 West 50th Street, Minneapolis
(612) 825-3201
$$

PANE VINO DOLCE delivers on its promise—bread, wine, and sweets—plus a whole lot more, operating from its tiny, virtually unmarked storefront in Linden Hills. The best way to spot the place is by the throngs outside the door hoping for a table. These prized seats are tightly packed against two long walls, making for a dining experience wherein you get to know your neighbors

FRANKLIN STREET BAKERY

1020 East Franklin Avenue • Minneapolis • (612) 879-5730

This may be the sunniest corner on East Franklin; indisputably, it's the tastiest. Rather than mirror the quaint aura of a little neighborhood bakery that's been around forever, Franklin Street celebrates its squeaky-clean surrounding in a spacious new edifice housing an operation that supplies many local restaurants (including Goodfellow's, owned by the same parent company) and supermarkets as well as a brisk walk-in trade. Patrons can peek through the window to survey a counter crammed with muffins, Danishes, doughnuts, croissants, scones, cookies, and more. Racks of bread (such as cranberry and wild rice, ciabatta, and honey-oat), buns, and fancy cakes to go add to the artworks on display. Coffee drinks are available, too.

almost as well as your own companion. With few soft surfaces to muffle the vivace noise level, conversations must be conducted fortissimo. But all voices hush at sundown, the magic moment when the candle-powered chandelier is lowered and reverently lit.

Pane Vino Dolce comes closest to being a true Italian trattoria in the cities. On the small, frequently changing menu designed by the chef/co-owner in his shoebox-sized kitchen, everything is made in-house, from the husky Tuscan bread to dip in vintage olive oil to the smooth-as-silk gelato.

The antipasti echo Italy, all right: crostini richly spread with mushrooms, a snappy olive tapenade, and roasted pepper and walnut paste, for example. Or bruschetta topped in classical fashion with tomatoes, basil, garlic, and olive oil. The Caesar salad is gutsy as all get-out, and the roasted beet edition is crowned with tangy Gorgonzola. Waiters push the pecorino offering—Swiss chard packets filled with that cheese melding truffles and porcini—and they know what they're talking about.

Four pizzas are available, splendid for sharing, each lush with quality in-gredients. Next comes the pasta listing, another option worthy of a Tuscan kitchen, such as penne in Gorgonzola cream spiced with pepper flakes, garlic, and walnuts or ravioli plump with chicken, pine nuts, raisins, ricotta, and rosemary. And the carefully stirred risotto, often laced with shellfish, is a perennial winner. So is the juniper-marinated bits of lamb that dot another plate of penne, in tandem with tomato and a touch of cream.

Entrées are limited to three: a chicken, a fish, and a meat preparation of the day. After all that has preceded the entrées, many patrons opt to share a single selection—that is, if they can narrow the choices down to one.

Because desserts are to be considered, too. And then there's a cup of espresso, followed by a glass of vin santo with biscotti at its side for dipping. Pane Vino Dolce's wines are displayed along the café's plate rail but are not listed. It's the servers' jobs to detail the select offerings of the day. To avoid sticker shock, it's wise to ask the price before making a commitment.

Neighborhood dwellers have adopted the café as their local hangout. It's a place where they can be assured of a good, honest, and delicious meal while greeting friends, who, by now, include the whole staff of the lively enterprise. The same group also has opened a French-influenced alternative, Cave Vin.

PRIMA

5325 Lyndale Avenue South, Minneapolis
(612) 827-7376
$–$$; F

THE ITALIAN NAME translates as "first," and that's the place this sweet little café holds in the hearts of its devotees. Located in a south Minneapolis neighborhood, the café is a charmer, with a cozy but slick setting and owners on-site, laboring in the trenches, not sitting in a corporate office somewhere on the coast. And patrons adore the simple but inviting menu of Cal-Ital fare that's notably long on freshness and short on price.

The interior, manicured with mocha paint and bisected by tall, charcoal-toned pillars, is a modern take on a diner, with a long row of counter stools facing the bustling open kitchen (providing the bonus of a cooking class with the price of your dinner, provided you can stop slurping spaghetti long enough to pay attention). Another row of stools lines a street-side counter for those intent on inspecting South Lyndale's passing parade. Or choose a two-top with leatherlike banquettes, well-lit by dangling ceiling lamps and well-attended by friendly servers.

The café is the first-born of Jennifer Jackson-King and Eliot King, who have gone on to open Three Fish in Calhoun Village and Big Buck in Minnetonka. Jennifer's forte is the front of the house, while Eliot is the guru behind the menu.

Pasta is primo at Prima, in variations ranging from a simple capellini with fresh basil, tomatoes, garlic, and Parmesan to penne con pollo alla Gorgonzola—grilled chicken breast, wild mushrooms, roasted peppers, and toasted walnuts in a garlic cream sauce, along with hand-rolled artisan lasagna and gnocchi as light as Ping-Pong balls, mined with spinach, peas, and Italian sausage in a roasted-tomato cream.

Several secondi are listed for those who relish dining in courses (or who can sweet-talk a neighbor into subdividing several plates). Grilled chicken risotto is a standard, laced with vegetables and a balsamic demi-glace, as is salmon atop garlic mashed potatoes, served with a portobello salsa and lemon butter. A husky rib eye has found its way to the menu, too.

Start with antipasti such as crispy crab cakes dolled up with a tomato-olive salsa and sauced with creamy leeks, or calamari wearing a spicy cornmeal crust atop a green-onion salad. Salads segue from Caesar, Caprese, and a toss of Italian chopped comestibles to a richly configured mix of grilled vegetables.

Panini, popular at lunch, elevates the workaday sandwich to an art form, with originals like roast beef layered with brie, spinach, and caramelized onions or a Tuscan chicken salad served on focaccia that's bursting with portobellos, caramelized onions, fresh mozzarella, and fontina; all arrive with a freshly tossed side salad.

The wine list is both affordable and accessible, as are a quartet of desserts, including a pumpkin bread pudding and a brown sugar/almond caramel cake, served with blueberry compote and vanilla bean gelato.

Romanticists bump elbows with "cook no more" boomers in the frequent wait for tables. But the magazine rack at the hostess stand is packed with back issues of *The Wine Spectator* to thumb for inspiration until your name is called.

RICE PAPER

2726 West 43rd Street, Minneapolis
(612) 926-8650 • ricepaperrestaurant.com
$; F; no reservations; no alcohol

IF YOUR MOTHER taught you that good things come in small packages, it's just possible she had Rice Paper in mind. The tiny Vietnamese restaurant in Linden Hills is somewhat larger than your average dining room table, but not much. It accommodates about two dozen customers at any given time, and therefore doesn't accept reservations. But its passionately loyal patrons don't seem to mind

INGEBRETSEN'S

1601 East Lake Street • Minneapolis • (612) 729-9331
www.ingebretsens.com

Ingebretsen's is a little bit of the Old Country in south Minneapolis, offering generations of Scandinavians a taste of home. When it opened its doors as a meat market and more back in 1921, it anchored the heart of the Swedish community. Today its near neighbors are Asian delis and Mexican taquerias, making this stretch of East Lake Street an even more exciting cultural stew. Folks swarm to Ingebretsen's for baked specialties—Swedish limpa, Danish kringle, and breads like Oslo rye. During the holiday season, especially, lines are three-deep at the meat counter, where Swedish meatballs, pâtés, sausages, specialty cheeses, fruit soup, pea soup, lingonberries, and brown beans are in special demand, along with herring in a rainbow of sauces, beef roast, fresh chickens, and, love it or leave it, lutefisk. "Anybody need help? Anybody beyond help?" joke the butchers as they package up pigs' feet and cabbage salad. An adjoining store sells tabletop and gift items from Scandinavia, too.

the wait at the height of the dinner rush, and once it's your turn, the food speeds swiftly from the kitchen.

The storefront's décor is composed of a spare, serene sea of pale green, shadowed with a motif of bamboo forests and living plants. Overseen by white paper lanterns, this oasis is as calm and tastefully composed as its owner, An Nguyen. (Those with long memories may recall her original Vietnamese café, the stylish Matin, which flourished for years in the Warehouse District.)

Matin's delicate spring rolls return here—cylinders of translucent rice paper wrapping bean sprouts, rice noodles, and a protein of your choice (chicken, tofu, or shrimp) with abundant bouquets of Thai basil, coriander, and mint. Or start with a pale pink fusion of eastern and western grapefruits, artfully arranged with bits of shrimp and pac peo, a nutty, minty herb. One feels closer to the Mekong than the Mississippi with the meal-sized Delta Bowl soup, wherein rice noodles tangle with pineapple, tomato, and more fresh herbs in a light lemongrass/garlic shrimp broth livened with lime.

An's entrées, all lightly portioned and picturesque enough for a photo shoot, pay homage to the traditional fare of her homeland, such as her Vietnamese rice noodle salad and a rustic Roadside Smoky Plate, a dish inspired by the roadside vendors she recalls from childhood, composed of aromatic grilled tofu rolled in ginger sauce and her favorite green herbs. Others are reinvented versions of a classic, such as the Rice Paper pad Thai, here lightened and highlighted by the yin-yang contrast of warm chicken or tofu and cool noodles, the crunch of peanuts with slithery Chinese mushrooms, and spicy garlic playing against refreshing lime.

Particularly comforting is her rice plate, Saigon-style. Chicken marinated in a lemongrass-oyster sauce, sprinkled with the fresh peanuts that seem to be the kitchen's fillip on many a dish, is served well by a scoop of jasmine rice. The aromatic rice also accompanies the popular coconut shrimp.

Meals are eased along with cups of jasmine tea and often end with a tall, cool class of iced coffee, Vietnamese-style, sweetened with condensed milk. At present, no desserts are on the menu (nor has a wine and beer license materialized), but those who swear by sweets can amble just up the block to Sebastian Joe's for exceptional ice cream.

TEJAS

3910 West 50th Street, Edina
(612) 926-0800 • www.tejasrestaurant.com
$$; F; P; O

DEEP IN THE HEART of Edina after its move from its original location downtown years ago, Tejas still shines as the star of the Southwestern dining scene. Celebrating the cooking styles and flavors of the American Southwest, it playfully teases the palates of those who grew up without chili, cumin, and mole to liven their dinners. The kitchen's crew loves to explore the smoky, sweet-to-spicy flavors that a repertoire of lively peppers can bring to a dish. But trust them as connoisseurs of subtle blendings, too—no incendiary explosions that require the paramedics.

As chefs come and go over the years, they've wisely kept the menu's classics firmly in place. The black-and-white bean soup still arrives, ladled with utmost care, a yin-yang of colors in a single bowl. Nor has anyone dared touched the Southwestern Caesar salad, since day one topped with generous shavings of Texan asiago cheese and cayenne croutons. The smoked chicken nachos, another don't-you-dare-change-it appetizer, still stand the test of time.

Yet new touches ease their way onto the menu, too, such as lobster-papaya quesadillas that add a Caribbean spin to the list of starters, as does a smoked-scallop seviche. Guacamole, fabricated at tableside, and barbecued pork tamales hie closer to the Texas border.

Segueing to heartier fare, the entrée list bristles with husky offerings to please carnivores: braised lamb shank with blue-corn "gnocchi" and a mint-cilantro sauce or hickory-grilled hanger steak, served fajita-style. Seafood offerings include the pan-roasted mahimahi, served with a sweet potato and manchego cheese taco and curried pineapple salsa.

Desserts are no mere afterthought in this kitchen. Consider chocolate fritters slathered with fiery fudge sauce (yes, those potent peppers work just fine here, too) or pear-cranberry crisp, served warm with ginger ice cream. Tejas proffers a cache of dozens of tequilas, available in tasting portions as well as single shots, and hand-squeezes a mighty mean lime margarita to enjoy in this casual setting, which is laced with quirky, tongue-in-cheek artifacts that brighten the adobe walls. There's a Navajo-style oven in the corner to set the mood for relaxation, and a wood grill that gilds the meats and veggies with chevrons of toasty brown, thrilling the suburban devotees who congregate here. People stop by to mingle with friends, catch a stylish bite before the movie playing across the street, or as a break from patrolling the upscale boutiques at this intersection. Brunch is a new addition, while special prix fixe wine dinners are long-standing red-letter days on many a fan's calendar.

CHAPTER FIVE

Downtown Saint Paul

A REBOURS

410 Saint Peter Street, Saint Paul
(651) 665-0656
$$

THE OWNER'S NAME is Anderson, the consulting chef is Swedish, but they pulled it off: A Rebours feels like it's a longtime denizen of the Left Bank of the Seine, not on the banks of the Mississippi in downtown Saint Paul. The bistro's look is vintage Paris all the way, from the tiny, prim tiles lining the floor to the lofty ceiling. The café is authentically tiny, too. A mere handful of banquettes and freestanding tables, where posies bloom and candles shimmer, line the dark wainscoting below walls of muted gold, hung with arresting modern art works—the kind that appeal to the trained eye of a collector like Doug Anderson.

The café has long been a twinkle in his eye, almost since he opened the equally small and equally successful Bakery on Grand in Minneapolis. When a sweet opportunity came his way at last, he was quick to sign the dotted line. About that time, Aquavit, the noted Swedish restaurant in Minneapolis, retreated to New York; but its Swedish chef de cuisine, Roger Johnsson, was enticed to act as menu consultant for the new project, which he visits regularly as seasonal menus change. Anderson also signed on Michael Morse, a "personality" maître d' of renown around town, to head up the front of the house.

With talent like this and a prize location on what's become the city's downtown restaurant row, success seemed assured. True to predictions, the bistro has been packed since its opening in summer 2004. Saint Paulites were quick to embrace it, patrons of the nearby Ordway Theater welcomed its arrival, and other metro foodies soon found their way to its door.

Servers, wearing towels knotted as aprons, are quick to deliver bread— hearty slices from the Minneapolis Bakery rather than ubiquitous baguettes. The menu they next present is short and fine-tuned: a single soup, for instance, such as a potage of butternut squash with bacon fritters, sage oil, and Spanish almonds. Or a pair of salads: simple greens tossed in a honey-lime dressing along with roasted garlic and spicy walnuts, or a tumble of pears, blue cheese, and port wine croutons over greens.

Hors d'oeuvres are stunningly simple, too—a sextet of plates that includes oysters on the half-shell with a Bloody Mary granita, a plate of charcuterie garnished with cornichons and olives, and Johnsson's silky, lime-cured salmon gravlax brightened with fresh oranges.

127

Entrees—six in all, and frequently changing—may segue from daintily elegant to elegantly hearty: basil-glazed scallops served upon ratatouille, monkfish with truffled polenta and haricots verts, a husky lamb cassoulet, steak au poivre with cognac sauce, and roasted veal tenderloin paired with a side of sublime mashed potatoes.

And there are five desserts. Well, four and a handsome plate of cheese. The chocolate cake has hazelnuts, crème fraiche, and strawberry sorbet on its platter; the profiteroles, plump with ice cream, flaunt a drizzle of chocolate; and the fig bread pudding wears a topknot of honey and cinnamon-crisp ice cream.

Coffee? Mais oui. Or more wine. The list is interesting, eclectic, and offered at fair value.

CASPERS' CHEROKEE SIRLOIN ROOM

886 Smith Avenue South, West Saint Paul
(651) 457-2729 • cherokeesirloin.com
$$; F

THE CHEROKEE SIRLOIN ROOM is caught in a time warp. It's the kind of a restaurant a business school would teach folks how to invent, if only they knew how. But it's tough to capture an inbred service ethic on an overhead projector or to clone the brand of warmhearted hospitality that makes you feel like long-lost kin the moment you walk in the door. And the food? Retro enough to make a modern marketing guru throw in his napkin.

Not a drop of balsamic vinegar in the kitchen, nor have the health food police got wind of the place—so, until it's raided, guests can eat their fill of cheese-draped au gratin potatoes, fat-rimmed beef, and deep-fried onion rings.

It's the Casper clan itself, now into the third generation of hands-on ownership, that keeps customers coming back to the blue-collar neighborhood supper club, located across the High Bridge from downtown Saint Paul. Opened as the Cherokee Café in 1934, the joint changed hands in 1972 when Bob and Dorothy Casper began the family's food dynasty. These days two sons, Rick and Jim, plus eight grandkids are involved, including the college lad who stops by to inquire, "Everything cooked to your liking?" His is the only suit and tie in a room filled with open collars and satin bowling jackets.

The career waitresses have been around almost as long as the setting of faux-leather booths and vintage photos. They're of the breed that call you "hon" as they deliver a basket of cellophane-wrapped crackers and an old-style relish tray. Other appetizers include giant onion rings, beer-battered frog legs, breaded mushrooms, breaded chicken tenders, and, for those who sincerely believe there's no tomorrow, a killer combo of ribs and onion rings.

Although there's a tasty salmon and a chicken on the menu, the place is a paean to beef. The cut the Caspers have dubbed the Steak of the Millennium is the best-seller—a top sirloin, cut extra-thick and weighing in at a full pound. It's ruddy and almost as easy to slice as butter. Rick Casper's personal favorite is the bone-in rib eye, at 24 ounces as burly as a fullback. It offers more flavor but less tenderness than the sirloin. And both are offered at prices that have hardly crept up over the decades.

And while we're on the subject of delicious excess, let's mention those famous au gratin potatoes. Sure, you can order your spuds baked or mashed, just as you can order the fruit plate for dessert at the Cheesecake Factory. But the reason even vegetarians elbow their way through the crowds waiting for a table is the Cherokee's famous dish, with more cheese and cream than cubes of flaky spuds and broiled till near-mahogany.

The dinner salad is not so innocent, either. It's a dish of standard greens drenched in what our parents would call "French" dressing—the brilliant orange kind—strewn with boulders of seductively salty blue cheese. With doggie bags as big as sacks from Nordstrom's, who wants to think about dessert?

This is the kind of old-style steakhouse where people order real drinks—and that doesn't mean a trendy Cosmo: We're talking Jim Beam and Jack Daniels. But it's easy to find a value-priced red on the wine list. You want a first-growth Bordeaux, go back to the other side of the river with your bank loan. Come here, instead, for a down-home good time.

FHIMA'S

6 West 6th Street, Saint Paul
(651) 287-0784 • www.fhimas.com
$$; M; valet parking

NO ONE EVER accused David Fhima of lacking style. His first club, Mpls Café, is as easy to look at as the classy young clientele who have voted it their clubhouse for dining, drinking, and dancing the night away.

When he opened his second supper club, he bestowed on downtown Saint Paul the same kind of sizzle. Fhima's is the club of the moment in these parts—and many moments to come. The showplace of the city, it could be equally at home in New York or L.A.

129

EL BURRITO MERCADO

175 Concord Street • Saint Paul • (651) 227-2192

It's more than a market, it's a clubhouse—a vibrant meeting place for the long-established Mexican community of Saint Paul's West Side. Pinatas mark the entrance to the mercado's cantina, where brightly painted chairs overflow with three generations of the market cum gossip center's regular patrons, who make themselves right at home. The cantina's cafeteria lineup makes ordering easy for gringos, too. Simply point, smile, and pay (very little). The market also boasts a more extensive deli section of takeout fare, ranging from meal-sized soups, salads, and aromatic hot dishes to sweet Mexican desserts. And beyond stretches a labyrinth of aisles stocked with ingredients—fresh or packaged and imported—with which to try your own hand.

A brushed-steel arch above the blue-lit entrance sets the tone for cool. Then, pass along the inner ramp and bam! you come to the bar. Scattered beyond are smooth white cocktail tables before a performance stage, also backlit in neon blue. Follow the burnt-orange carpet past the lofty, glassed-in wine room (and its single private dining alcove) to banquettes deluxe, where reclining is made easy with velvet pillows against a wall of faded blue. They offer first-class viewing of the open, industrial-style kitchen, all shining steel—except the bright-tiled façade of the woodburning oven, topped with Fhima's signature "F."

Servers, dressed head to toe in midnight blue, deliver menus that meld the French and North African culinary icons of this chef-owner's heritage. Thus, start the evening with pommes frites and a rich slab of foie gras if that's your fancy, or vote for a sampling of Moroccan tapas: hummus, roasted peppers, almond goat cheese, eggplant marmalade, and more, to slather over rosemary focaccia.

Salads, too, leap the Mediterranean, with a French salade Niçoise next to a Moroccan-influenced Caesar. Entrées take a similar stand: the dazzling fish list includes a concoction of date trout with roasted almonds, swordfish with polenta and tomatoes, halibut Catalan, and sole Malaga. Fhima also offers a proper steak béarnaise (augmented with a sweet-potato soufflé) and tosses chicken in his pot-au-feu.

Yet it's on the list marked "specialties" where the kitchen provides fare few others in town are doing: truly Moroccan tagines of pork, lamb, or fish; couscous; a seafood paella; and authentic bouillabaisse.

Fhima knows his wines—760 labels and counting, flaunted on a Vegas-style wine wall. Cocktails also go over well here with the after-work crowd and those tripping in later for salsa dancing or the sounds of Latin jazz. It's close enough to the Ordway Theater to capture that audience, too. And what could be a more stylish setting for a business lunch?

PAZZALUNA

360 Saint Peter Street, Saint Paul
(651) 223-7000 • pazzaluna.com
$$–$$$; valet parking; O

THEY CALL THEMSELVES "urban Italian," and that's right on the money. So is the translation of the moniker "Pazzaluna"—a chef that goes wild when crazed by the moon. The kitchen also heralds the old Italian saying, inscribed on the dining room wall, "A tavola, nessun diverta vecchio"—at the table, no one grows old. So as if any lure were needed beyond the pleasing fare from Northern Italy, that maxim is one to consider.

This downtown Saint Paul ristorante, a leading player in "the Rice Park restaurant district," highlights the best architectural elements of a vintage structure that also shimmers with the high style of today. Thus, the original mammoth central pillars still stand, and a wall of windows that capture the sunlight for luncheon diners are shaded with—what else?—Venetian blinds. A soft, dark carpet and draperies the color of Chianti help dress up the sea of crisp white tablecloths surrounded by ladder-back chairs.

The street-side bar offers a contemporary setting for the meet-and-mingle crowd at the end of a business day, or to precede or conclude an Ordway Theater performance. Behind the bar, a repro of Botticelli's famous Venus "on the half-shell" occupies the entire back wall.

To the rear stretches a counter with diner stools, where patrons can order in full view of the antics of the busy kitchen. In fact, the cooks have been known to send out surprise samples to these ardent voyeurs. Those who prefer more private surroundings for business dinners or social celebrations can head to the back room, which has a racy mural depicting the glory days of Saint Paul in the Roaring Twenties.

No matter where guests are seated, soon they'll be on their feet again to inspect the antipasti counter, where selections change nightly based on the chef's whim. Or they can select from the standard menu's starters, which include bruschetta rustica, topped with the traditional tomatoes, basil, and olive oil; steamed mussels rich with garlic; slabs of the kitchen's homemade mozzarella stuffed with prosciutto di Parma; or beef carpaccio in the thinnest slices the adept carver can produce.

If soup or salad is your first-course choice, pasta e fagiole, rich with white beans and orzo, makes a swell beginning, as does the shepherd's salad, a rustic toss of salami, chick peas, olives, and tomatoes, all served in a Parmesan shell. And when in Rome, it's always good to order a Caesar.

Pizza from the woodburning oven is of the rippling, thin-crust variety; choose from a half-dozen toppings. Or proceed to the list of pasta, gnocchi, and risotto, where the kitchen truly shines. But leave room, as your server will caution, for entrées such as Gorgonzola-stuffed beef loin, smoked pork chop served with cherry-apricot chutney, veal scaloppini served three ways, and seafood like pancetta-wrapped salmon in tomato pesto.

Nor does the dessert list let you off lightly. There's a fine selection of Italian (and other) wines. And did we mention the homemade bread to swipe through that green-gold olive oil?

RUAM MIT

475 Saint Peter Street, Saint Paul
(651) 290-0067 • ruammitthai.com
$–$$; F

DON'T LET THE RATHER seedy stretch of Saint Peter Street in downtown Saint Paul deceive you. This storefront café conjures up some of the very best Thai food in the twin towns. Aficionados of this liveliest of Asian cuisines know this, and they have helped keep Ruam Mit popular for years. In appearance the restaurant could stand in for a cheery, small-town coffee shop, with two small rooms innocuously done up in blond wainscoting, white walls, hanging warehouse lights, and Formica-topped booths and tables. While a few Thai artifacts add to the décor, the true touches of the homeland are saved for what comes out from the kitchen.

Owner S. Vongkhamdeng calls his place "the House of Pad Thai," and he's not far wrong. That appealing, meal-size bowl of soup-stew comfort fare anchors a menu that leads off with star appetizers: egg rolls and spring rolls;

chicken and pork satay skewers; chicken wings stuffed with pork, black mushrooms, and translucent thread noodles, served with the kitchen's homemade sweet-and-sour sauce; and crispy curry puffs gilded with crushed peanuts. Or summon the do-it-yourself mi eng kum platter of lettuce and wrap up ingredients such as dried shrimp, lemon, ginger, jalapeno peppers, onion, and toasted coconut.

Many followers swear by Ruam Mit's tom yum soup, livened with kaffir lime, red curry paste, and potent little Thai chilies. Or proceed straight to the red curry dishes themselves, with choice of beef, chicken, duck, or fish. Fans of yellow curry are seldom disappointed, and it would also be a mistake to overlook the chili crab, the closest thing to the Far Eastern version to be found in these Midwestern parts. The same goes for the addictive, tart-sweet green papaya salad.

Pad Thai is just the leader of a long list of rice and noodle dishes in which to add the protein of your predilection. Desserts herald the standard Thai favorites: Thai custard and sweet-and-sticky rice, even better when embellished with mango. And while the bubble tea craze prevails, it's also offered here.

SAINT PAUL GRILL

350 Market Street, Saint Paul
(651) 224-7455 • stpaulgrill.com
$$$; valet parking

ASK SAINT PAULITES where they make their reservations for a big night out (or even ask their Minneapolis neighbors, who sneak across the river in search of a good time), and chances are stupendous that they'll all name the Saint Paul Grill. The dining room of the Saint Paul Hotel took the city by storm from the moment it first opened decades ago, and the thunder hasn't abated to this day.

Part of the magic is in the setting, with windows that capture the charm of Rice Park and the Ordway Theater across the way. Inside, it feels like Old Saint Paul—a warmly traditional clubhouse of low ceilings shepherding private-as-you-please dark wood booths topped with frosted glass. The small cluster of tables at the entrance are where the movers and shakers are known to sit—legislators, bankers, and the "name" performers at the Ordway, who often turn up ravenous after the show. (There's also a rotunda-like room in the rear.) These tables are dressed for dining and dealing—devoid of flowers and candles but loaded with bottles of condiments and a notepad to record the deals being cut.

Many a regular prefers to eat in the adjoining bar, however, a manly setting with a wooden floor, black tables, and the awe-inspiring bar itself, backed by a wall of premium bottles. The bar menu is served until the wee hours, when most other kitchens have called it a night.

The list walks the line between steakhouse style—grill it, serve it—and a chef-driven kitchen where invention lures diners into the door. Thus, the Grill serves a mighty mean crab cake, but sends it out on a bed of spinach with a side of lemon-tarragon aioli. It cures and smokes its salmon in the classic manner, serves it with the traditional accompaniments, then adds a lime-caper cream sauce as an understated fillip. Again, the cream of wild rice soup follows classic routes, while the chicken noodle version shimmers with an extra shake of pepper. On a popular salad plate, pears, walnuts, and blue cheese mingle, as on many another menu, but here they're personalized with a honey-walnut vinaigrette.

People flock here for red meat, no bones about it. And the Grill lives up to its promise with prime cuts, like a New York strip, sliced into full-pound servings; a filet mignon half that size, sauced with a Pinot Noir shallot butter; a bone-in rib eye the menu touts as "the original cowboy steak"; and a grilled rib eye of bison, too. And yes, the Grill is justly famous for its liver, served just as you'd expect it, alongside plenty of bacon and onions. Yet fish gets equal billing here, and the pan-fried walleye leads the list of favorites.

This is the place for traditional "sides." The walk-away winner is the Grill's au gratin potatoes, topped with a blend of cheddar and Parmesan. The fries are hand-fashioned from Idahoes, while baby reds are the fodder for the mountains of mashed potatoes, whipped into clouds with buttermilk and sour cream.

Servers seem to possess skills in mind reading, which means your private conversations—business or pleasure—take precedence over a relentless recitation of the list of specials. These vets and vets-in-training are skilled at moving the evening along at their patrons' pace, whether it's to catch the theater's curtain or linger over dessert.

SAKURA

350 Saint Peter Street, Saint Paul
(651) 224-0185 • sakurastpaul.com
$$; P

FOLKS LOVED SAKURA when it was just a hole in the wall on a path generally unbeaten. Getting started, proprietress Joyce Omari warmly welcomed sushi lovers of all persuasions, from Twin Cities devotees of Japan's best-loved edible art to business visitors from Tokyo longing for a taste of home.

Then Joyce moved uptown to busier Saint Peter Street and a bigger, brighter location that's easier to spot. Next, in the autumn of 2004, she expanded her attractive site, annexing space and undertaking a renovation that includes new balcony seating and an enlarged sushi bar. Mammoth windows anchor a design with a relaxed, minimalist air that's a masterpiece of understatement. Vast, uncluttered surfaces in muted tones of grape, avocado, tobacco, and tangerine act as backdrop for the sushi bar, tended by chefs in paper caps who adroitly fashion sushi and sashimi before the eyes of palpitating diners. Oversized blackboards list the scores of fresh seafood that go into those tiny, pristine bites.

As for the morsels themselves, they're the best in Saint Paul, as attested by Joyce's countrymen placing order after order at the sushi bar. Choose from favorites such as tuna, halibut, striped bass, mackerel, and many other varieties of seafood, including shrimp, squid, clams, scallops, eel, sea urchin, flying fish, and salmon roe. Some cannot help but make an entire meal of Sakura's sushi. Sashimi—sushi without the rice—is just as fresh.

Those seeking more elaborate appetizers are partial to the battered oysters, green mussels on the half-shell, soft-shell crabs, or marinated short ribs. Others have become addicted to munching on the edamame (soy beans that resemble lima beans, but they're tastier).

Seaweed salad (or a simple toss of garden greens) clears the palate for Omari's lengthy list of entrées, ranging from the familiar and well-loved sukiyaki, teriyaki, and tempura to shabu shabu, a beef and vegetable dish cooked tableside in seasoned broth, plus a pair of bento samplers. The yakizakana offerings appeal to connoisseurs of this salted and broiled fish preparation, with fillets accented by freshly ground daikon radish.

Miso soup after the leisurely meal freshens the appetite for dessert. Typically Japanese, they're simple: sweet rice cake with red bean filling wrapped in an oak or cherry leaf; there's also the not so simple, and not so Japanese, deep-fried ice cream (the green tea and ginger flavors are particularly delicious).

Sake, served warm or cold, makes a good accompaniment to the chefs' handiwork, as does a cold mug of Japanese beer. Tea, of course, is replenished often by Sakura's discreet and polished servers.

CHAPTER SIX

Saint Paul's
Selby and Highland Neighborhoods

128 CAFÉ

128 Cleveland Avenue North, Saint Paul
(651) 645-4128 • 128cafe.net
$$

128 CAFÉ, named for its street address bordering the Saint Thomas College campus, succeeds despite its setting—or, some might say, because of it. The homey café, launched in the mid-90s, occupies the below-stairs level of a vintage apartment building, a site adapted from a former campus beer joint.

It's not much more pretentious these days. Done up in knotty pine, the space recalls the family rec room of years ago , or perhaps the gathering place of a northern lakes resort, comfy as an old shoe. Folks—diners and staff alike—feel at home here in their flannel shirts.

Then there's the food. That's what elevates this place to destination dining. The café is owned by husband-and-wife chefs Natalie and Brock Obee, who keep their seasonally influenced menu as unassuming as its setting. Together they hone a dinner-only menu of six entrées—beef, poultry, an occasional fish dish, and always something vegetarians can savor. Then they inject taste elements guaranteed to turn your head.

Roast chicken, for instance—the real kind, like the good old days—shares plate space with a carefully crafted artichoke and sweet pepper risotto. The pork du jour may borrow flavor from sour cherries and smoked bacon. Cuts of beef unite with lusty herbs under glazes infused with seasonal mushrooms, served with a hefty side of mashed potatoes—the true, home-cooked kind. More forward seasonings are found in dishes like linguine, which gets a gutsy little kick from curry and chipotle peppers, then tossed with leeks and golden raisins. And the ribs? Worth the drive alone.

Starters are conceived with equal parts of care and "well, why not?" Thus, a bulb of garlic, roasted till it melts, is sent out with a creamy slab of goat cheese and an apple-raisin-tomato chutney dancing with a hint of ginger. A salad of peppery arugula comes with flecks of beets, hazelnuts, and pungent blue cheese.

The café is a favorite for date nights, including outings for long-married couples. It's easy to relax over affordably priced wine and to linger on with coffee and one of the café's retro desserts. Bread pudding, for instance, comes laced with caramelized walnuts, while a crème brûlée calls on espresso to kick it up a notch.

Others make it a habit to head here for Sunday brunch, when omelets, crepes, and coffeecake warm from the oven take the stage, along with heartier fixings such as smoked pork chops or a little steak.

CAFÉ LATTE

850 Grand Avenue, Saint Paul
(651) 224-5687 • www.cafelatte.com
$; F; no reservations

IF IT CEASED to exist, well, there goes our touted quality of life. Since Peter and Linda Quinn introduced their new style of eating back in 1987, Café Latte has been Grand Avenue's hottest dining destination, all day long and well into the night. Many have tried to copy the concept and piggyback on its success, but they've failed to tap its magic. And Peter himself, though widely wooed, is astute enough to stake his claim as a restaurateur at a one-and-only location.

With vision, he remodeled a former auto dealership into two levels of table space, which offer vistas of the avenue's passing parade. Then he designed an attractive cafeteria-style short-order line to showcase the light, fresh, and tasty items devised by his wife, Linda, who heads up the kitchen.

AMORE

Milton Mall • 917 Milton Street • Saint Paul • (612) 222-6770

Amore fits that romantic image of a coffeehouse as a home away from home, suited up in castoffs from grandma's attic—that is, if grandma had the foresight to save her beaded lampshades and plush, overstuffed sofas. Textured stucco walls face others with wild, gay murals (think Chagall's lovers—that's Amore—holding a giant steaming cup of coffee). Marble tabletops host those beaded lamps as beacons in the shadows along the barista's counter. In the back, an alcove doubling as a private meeting room boasts a vintage bedroom dresser; close by, there's another cozy hideaway, a corner with sofas where you can enjoy your pick from the bookshelves. Needless to mention, the coffee's rich and strong and good. Specialties like Mexican mocha and Café Cubano liven the usual list. And in summertime, a shaded front porch provides a prime place for people-watching.

You'll always find a couple of daily-changing soups, the café's famous display of composed salads (best choice for the indecisive: the three-item sampler plate), sandwiches built to order on the kitchen's homemade bread, and a couple of stews, usually with a piquantly seasoned ethnic twist.

Designer coffee drinks are another specialty; in fact, back in the 80s, this café led the espresso charge along the avenue, putting Maxwell House to rest. Wine and beer also are available in token offerings.

But let's be honest: The big draw is the desserts. Wisely (or not), they're displayed in cases at the beginning of the cafeteria line, to enjoy here or take home. The kitchen's forte, guests claim, is its signature chocolate turtle cake, a hefty slice that's sweet and black as sin and almost as tall as the lofty ceiling. Others are partial to rich, New York–style cheesecakes, fruit tarts, mousses, or bundt cakes. Bread loaves, too, are positioned on display racks to entice willing customers.

Mezzanine seating is favored by tray-carriers who may have brought along paperwork to pore over during lunch or tea. The back room's tables, added to accommodate the perennially long lines, draw shoppers. And the storefront's sidewalk-facing seats, which disappear the fastest, are snatched up by everyone from soccer moms, stroller pushers, students from nearby campuses, and pre- and après-theater patrons lusting for a slice of cake to sweeten the performance.

DIXIES

695 Grand Avenue, Saint Paul
(651) 222-7345 • dixiesongrand.com
$$; P

Dixies Calhoun
Calhoun Beach Club, 2730 West Lake Street, Minneapolis
(612) 920-5000, dixiescalhoun.com
$$; O; F

THEY'RE WHISTLING UP and down Grand Avenue, and once you get a whiff of Dixies' Southern-style smokehouse barbecue, the reason is made clear. For over two decades these preachers of that ol' time religion of the kitchen have been signing on converts just as fast as those meaty slabs appear.

They're purists who do it the old-fashioned way, slow-smoking the stacks over hickory wood, then finishing them off with a run under the broiler to coat them with their trademark char-tinged crunch. Sauce, as barbeque connois-

DUNN BROS. COFFEE

1569 Grand Avenue • Saint Paul • (651) 698-0618

Dunn's locally founded mini-chain of coffeehouses now boasts multiple locations, but the original—opened in this Macalester College neighborhood in 1987—remains the mothership. It's funkier, for one thing. Stiff black church pews line the walls, which themselves do double duty as an art gallery. Chairs in vintage vinyl of lipstick red are pulled to round black tables, customarily strewn with newspapers, textbooks, laptop computers, and other signs that this is almost an official campus hangout. The storefront's window serves as a stage for the live music offered late each evening. But coffee is still the main attraction. It couldn't be fresher, for the roaster dominates the rear of the room and perfumes the whole arena.

seurs demand, is served on the side, never slapped on the meat while it's cooking. That job is left to each individual member of the 'cue congregation; some stay firm in their faith in the smooth, original recipe, while others, who have seen the light, have strayed to the spicier shack version. Either way, with an order of the baby backs or country-style rib chops, you're assured of the traditional fixings—homemade baking powder biscuits so light they threaten to levitate, skin-on fries with lots of creamy Southern gravy, and corn on the cob. The barbecued chicken and Cajun-spiced pork chops (or combos of the above) merit the same add-ons, along with TLC on the smoker.

Say you can't stomach Southern barbecue? Well, heaven help you, and Dixies will, too. Folks can start their feast with homemade beef jerky, cornmeal-coated catfish nuggets, or a cup—if you can stop at that—of the kitchen's Cuban black bean soup, Louisiana gumbo, or choice of Dixies' award-winning chili (waver between the chicken version or Pecos Red River style). "Just" a salad? No such thing. The most popular plate of greens comes topped with fried chicken in a honey-mustard dressing.

Just a sandwich? Okay, that works. The "shack" number favors lean pulled pork; or choose Southern-fried walleye (talk about fusion cooking), the Cajun burger, or the catfish club. Po'boys are a house specialty, too.

Dixies' dinner menu also features chicken-fried steak, Kentucky bourbon pot roast, Carolina crab cakes, and authentic jambalaya, served with corn bread. And those Southern brothers sure do know how to favor a sweet tooth. Dixies' baker is famous for his key lime pie as well as those luscious slices of butterscotch pecan, while the white chocolate bread pudding won't send you home hungry, either.

While the food is down-home delicious, the setting's been gentrified. Expect a grand-scale version of Cheers, centered around a huge, octagonal bar, above which a papier-mâché alligator—clearly an émigré from Carnivale—hovers.

The Calhoun cousin of Dixies brings these treats across the river from the original to the shores of Lake Calhoun, with a view provided along with outdoor seating in summer as well as a slightly more upscale setting. The Southern brunch served family-style—with all of the above fixings, and more—should leave you satiated until the next Lord's Day rolls around again. Each month, Dixies salutes a different state of the Deep South with specially featured soups, salads, entrées, and desserts.

THE GREEN MILL

57 Hamline Avenue South, Saint Paul
(651) 698-0353 • greenmill.com
$$; F

Ten additional metro locations

THIS IS WHERE it all got started. Today the Green Mill's many satellites rule the local pizza world, yet none can match the easygoing ambience of the original location. The enterprise was launched back in the 80s by Macalester College students Brian and Chris Bangs—a couple of kids who clearly could teach their profs a thing or two about running a dramatically successful business.

The perky green neon above the entrance is about all that's been added over the years. Within, it's still a casual collage of fake-wood paneled walls (hung with dozen of real awards for winning pizza), multiple TV screens, booths big enough for six or eight hungry worshipers of the art form that these boys have perfected, and a sea of tables. There's also seating at the crowded bar counter, and even a sister store adjoining the Mill, dedicated to takeout orders. That arena's got plenty of tables, too, empty when there's a 30-minute wait next door: same great product, but scrubbed of atmosphere.

Waiters in the black T-shirts that serve as uniforms do their best to squeeze along the narrow spaces between seats and navigate the clots of hopeful customers congregating at the entrance, determined to wait it out for a space.

The clientele is a microcosm of the neighborhood: three-generation families, old married couples escaping their kitchens, college kids on date night, and whoever else is either lucky enough to live nearby or willing to fight for a parking space within sprinting distance.

The Mill's pizza ovens turn out three kinds of crusts. Choose the classic flat-style, a hand-tossed pescara—the most popular—or a deep-dish version, à la Chicago. The sauce is rich with tomatoes and spices and painted on lavishly, and the cheese is of quality. The usual toppings are offered, and some not so usual, like goat cheese, sun-dried tomatoes, and prosciutto. Stuffed pizzas and calzones provide the same litany of design options.

Yes, there's life beyond pizza here these days. Years ago the Mill expanded its menu to include an interesting list of pastas—fettucine puttanesca, linguine primavera, three-cheese lasagna, and more—as well as meal-sized salads, including a mango-pecan number and a chicken-walnut-spinach toss, plus a list of classic appetizers, such as chicken wings six ways. These, and a pitcher of beer, constitute a meal for many.

Others come for the burgers and still others for the pan-fried walleye, served with garlic potatoes, or one of the Mill's prime steaks. Desserts are listed, too, but with all else that's going on, it's hard to imagine why—until you taste the ancho diablo cake, sinful with chocolate and a fiery punch of chili peppers.

The Green Mill brews its own beer, both ales and lagers, right here on the premises (peek through the window to ogle the silvery vats and sacks of malt) and offers other labels, too, as well as a most respectable wine list.

HEARTLAND

1806 Saint Clair Avenue, Saint Paul
(651) 699-3536 • www.heartlandrestaurant.com
$$–$$$

HAVE YOU HEARD of the Slow Foods movement? It started in Rome to protest the opening of a McDonald's and has since spread throughout our country, too. Locally, squads of chefs are hanging their hats and hearts on re-educating diners in what food is all about—a sensory experience, an homage to the earth and its stewards rather than the factory. They'll serve you an heirloom tomato, sweet as candy and still warm from the sun, rather than those gas-ripened rocks picked while still green and trucked from wherever. Maybe you'll pay a little extra for the opportunity to support the small guy as well as the chance to feast on chicken free of steroids. Many diners swear it's well worth the tiny boost in price.

And that's what Heartland is all about. Chef-proprietor Lenny Russo, who's been cooking in many of the best kitchens in town for years, at last has launched his own café to showcase those principles while providing diners with his signature takes on the regional food to which he's committed (chance of seeing lobster on his menu: nil). Lenny provided the elbow grease to renovate a 1920s Mac-Groveland neighborhood storefront himself, using the clean, inviting air of Prairie School architecture as his model and positioning an open kitchen in view of the floor to further unite the food on your plate with how it got there.

He offers two ways to dine here: first, a pair of three-course prix fixe menus, one labeled "fauna," the other "flora." Meat eaters often dive for the former, savoring their way through an appetizer of, say, wild rice–crusted Lake Huron perch with heirloom tomato vinaigrette, then an entrée of Minnesota lamb roast served with fresh local flageolet beans, baby carrots, and house-cured smoked pork, with a wickedly dark chocolate crème brûlée for finale, served with a hickory nut shortbread cookie, black raspberry curd, and a sumac berry tuile.

Those relishing the "flora" list might find an heirloom tomato salad with pepper cress and Carr Valley Wisconsin blue cheese, followed by hand-cut North Dakota semolina wheat fettucine topped with local zucchini, onions, eggplant, and chanterelles at the height of their season. Then a Michigan blueberry tart arrives, accented with lavender caramel, vanilla custard sauce, and candied black walnuts.

Plan two is to peruse the à la carte list, where eager eyes can light on the likes of Minnesota bison tartare, an organic carrot-ginger soup, grilled antelope rib eye with patty pan squash and roasted heirloom garlic sauce, or sturgeon with baby bok choy and leek confit. Whatever your choice, an *amuse* as a gift from the chef precedes it, along with a basket of house-baked sourdough bread in nightly changing flavors.

Yes, Chef Russo wears his mission on the sleeve of his chef's whites, and the fans, who have followed him from restaurant to restaurant, are delighted to let him fly. In fact, many simply say, "Serve me," and wait for the surprise.

KHYBER PASS

1571 Grand Avenue, Saint Paul
(651) 690-0505
$–$$; F

KHYBER PASS MIGHT well serve as the poster model for a wishful diner's dream of a charming ethnic restaurant—the diner who seeks magic along with his meal. It's an escape, for an hour or two, to a "faraway" setting and a mini-slice of another culture with no frequent flier miles involved.

COOKS OF CROCUS HILL

977 Grand Avenue • Saint Paul • (651) 228-1333
Additional locations in Edina's 50th & France and Southdale

Cooks of Crocus Hill takes cooking seriously and provides all the wherewithal for amateurs and seasoned hosts alike to cook up a storm in their home kitchens. From utensils and tools of every imaginable use (and some that veer beyond sanity), baking and serving dishes, kitchen linens, and small appliances, on to cookbooks and special ingredients—fancy mustards, oils, vinegars, and lots more—this store provides deluxe one-stop shopping. And if recipes and advice are wanted, count on the words from the experienced staff. All the stores offer many classes headed by local restaurant chefs and visiting cookbook authors to further improve one's dinner parties or to simply graduate from frozen fare; kids' classes flourish, too.

The pretty brick storefront sets the stage, with trim gleaming under a fresh coat of robin's-egg blue and bright flowers spilling from the planters. Behind those cheerily painted doors, ivy tumbles from above. The foyer room, with a half-dozen tables framed by plants, captures sunlight from the street. Three graceful, pillared arches lead to the main dining room, a relaxed setting. Overhead, carpets in intricate patterns cover the ceiling, traditional festive garments sway above the hostess counter in the rear, and select artworks brighten the creamy yellow walls. Fans twirl lazily above, and birds in cages gently swing.

Green marble-toned tabletops are spaced to foster quiet, Muzak-free conversations. They're filled with a comfortable mix of faculty from Macalester College just across the intersection, neighborhood friends congregating to gossip with each other, and loyal fans who followed the Afghani owners from the former Saint Clair Avenue location a number of years ago.

The menu lists a dozen entrées, evenly divided among vegetarian, chicken, lamb, beef, and combination platters. Kebabs of chicken, served on a bed of basmati rice with chutney, or chicken in a curry sauce along with stewed potatoes and basmati, are typical Afghani dishes. Lovers of lamb will find it on a skewer; stewed with leeks and spinach or yellow lentils, onions, and garlic; or cooked with mung beans and chutney.

The appetizer list is even more enticing: bean soup laced with mint and yogurt, for instance, or leek dumplings; eggplant cooked with tomatoes or roasted with garlic and hot peppers; homemade hummus; and a choice of chutneys—walnut-cilantro or apricot fired with hot red peppers.

Desserts—only three—can cleanse and cool the palate with something sweet and creamy, such as milk pudding with cardamom, rose water, and a topping of pistachios, or rice pudding, also laced with rose water and cardamom and studded with a toss of walnuts. Or choose baklava, rich with nuts and honey.

Although a spare listing of wine and beer is offered, Afghani beverages are the forte here: green Afghani tea with cardamom; sweetened black tea with both cardamom and milk; or a refreshing drink of yogurt, cucumber, and mint. Service is as casual and friendly as if you were a guest in an Afghani home.

LA GROLLA

452 Selby Avenue, Saint Paul
(651) 221-1061
$$; O

LA DOLCE VITA comes to Selby Avenue in this stylish little café. Picture a glamorous, movie-set rendition of a romantic trattoria, and that's a snapshot of La Grolla. Several seasons ago, the *padrones* of the well-respected Tiramisu took over the failing Tulips location—a pretty site—and transformed it into an even more magical setting.

Within the vintage red brick storefront, dark wainscoting with walls of creamy brick, a slate-paneled floor, and far-reaching windows are just the beginning. Add sheer, billowing curtains tied back to capture the action on the street, a tiny, marble-topped bar just behind the hostess stand, a copper hood sheltering the open kitchen, and works of art in thick, complicated gilt frames, and it's easy to understand why one neighborhood couple after another pushes through the door in hopes of a table. And pretty tables they are, too, with their marble surfaces adorned with a blooming sprig.

An alcove behind the wine display captures a few more tables in a space that's quieter and roomier but a bit removed from the titillating bustle (and the chance to sneak a peek at what's on your neighbors' plates).

Chances are, their plates are piled with rounds of bruschetta loaded with mozzarella and tomatoes, a winner among the starters. Try the Caprese salad, composed in classic fashion with fresh mozzarella, tomatoes, basil, and a splash of the best balsamic vinegar or a platter of deep-fried calamari paired with lightly battered zucchini blossoms to dip in a spicy arrabiata sauce.

Pasta dishes follow, ranging from a simple, well-made angel hair tossed with fresh tomatoes, basil, and extra-virgin olive oil to penne in a vodka sauce; dainty gnocchi in a silky tomato cream sauce; ravioli stuffed with seafood; or lasagna della nonna ("grandma's style," and how can one go wrong with that?).

Seafood proves itself the forte of the entrée list, shining in dishes like grilled tuna served with a shiitake mushroom and rosemary sauce or salmon sauced in caramelized ginger. Osso buco, not always easy to find on an Italian menu in these parts, anchors the menu here, served with your (difficult) choice of polenta or risotto Milanese. There's an archetypal veal scaloppini too, and a couple of tricks the kitchen does with fowl, such as duck breast fanned out over poached radicchio leaves in a honey and balsamic vinegar sauce. And with a chef who formerly cooked at a place called Tiramisu, it's almost needless to add that you should save room for dessert.

Summertime brings the bonus of outdoor seating in La Grolla's leafy patio, sequestered from the traffic of the street by greenery. Lingering in the twilight with a glass of Pinot Grigio or tiny cup of strong espresso, *la vita* doesn't get much more *dolce* around here.

THE LEXINGTON

1096 Grand Avenue, Saint Paul
(651) 222-5878 • the-lexington.com
$$; P

THE LEX, as it's fondly called by anyone born and bred in Old Saint Paul, has been a Grand Avenue institution since 1935. And nothing much has changed in the ensuing decades, because what worked well then has stood the test of time. There's no fusion menu or newfangled décor here. Instead, the clubby Old English bar still draws graying gents whose letters from overseas in World War II were displayed there. (In return, they received a newsletter with tales from home.) State legislators informally caucus in the bar's shadows, and business cronies consider the place their club. Ladies still put on their hats for Sunday lunch, and teenagers routinely stop by in their finery en route to the prom. Many won't consider themselves married without a bridal shower in the dining room.

The waitstaff boasts scores of years of service, too; count on them to remember just how you like your steak or your martini. They confidently patrol the floor, from one corner of its French Provincial wood paneling to the other, under the glow of beaded chandeliers and gleaming gilt picture frames.

And the all-American cuisine has never wavered in its mission. The kitchen's tried-and-true menu highlights prime rib—the perennial favorite—as well as a popular rendition of lamb shanks simmered in red wine, liver and onions, and braised short ribs. These, and virtually every item that comes through the kitchen door, are made from scratch, from the secret house salad dressing to comforting, old-fashioned desserts like pecan pie.

The chicken liver pâté is a classic among the appetizers, along with the Minnesota wild rice soup. Escargot, prepared in the traditional manner with lots of garlic, vies with a reliable shrimp cocktail, served with homemade cocktail sauce, and crab cakes come with Dijon mustard on the side, just as the regulars love them.

None of this à la carte nonsense here—all entrées arrive fully dressed with a choice of homemade soup or the famous Lexington or Caesar salad, along with vegetables and freshly baked bread. The slow-roasted prime rib sells best, but the filet mignon and walleye amandine combo runs a close second. And some people swear this is the only place these days to get a decent chicken pot-pie or hot turkey dinner, complete with mashed potatoes, stuffing, cranberries, and gravy. Thus the grande dame of Grand Avenue continues to satisfy, rather than startle, its loyal neighborhood of regulars—a dining tradition passed on from generation to generation among Crocus Hill devotees.

LUCI ANCORA

2060 Randolph Avenue, Saint Paul
(651) 698-6889 • luciancora.com
$$–$$$

NO ROOM AT the inn—er, ristorante. That was the pleasant problem arising from the enduring success of Highland Park's cozy little Ristoranti Luci (see listing). Hemmed in by unyielding walls, where to expand? A more spacious catty-corner site provided a welcome answer, and *ecco*: Luci Ancora ("Luci Again") was born.

The seating capacity is much greater, but with the same warm but near-bare walls in hues of milky coffee, the same drapery swags (this time adorning far more windows), the same crisp white tablecloths with their votive candles, and the same lack of fuss and frills. People are drawn here to eat, and eat well, rather than by trendiness or fancy designer touches in the décor. (A working fireplace is an added plus, however, while the deli-cooler display of white wine is less easy on the eyes.)

Ancora swears by the same local and organic providers as its older sister, but here there's a bit more emphasis on seafood as the forte of the chef. Antipasti, therefore, lead off with grilled shrimp, often dolled up with spicy green beans, cashews, and sesame oil. Crostini topped with cream cheese, grilled apples, and toasted almonds under a drizzle of honey is another splendid starter. There are two classic, simple salads that call on excellent imported olive oil and Parmigiano Reggiano cheese.

First plates star linguine con gamberi—noodles served with wild rock shrimp, pine nuts, carrots, garlic, and hot pepper flakes. Risotto features peeky toe crab along with assorted vegetables amid the rice. Vegetarians savor pastas such as husky tubes of garganelli tossed with tomatoes, leeks, cream, and vodka.

Fish of the day leads the list of secondi, which also aims to please carnivores with beef served with grilled mushrooms and Gorgonzola, braised lamb shank atop saffron risotto, and Wild Acres chicken in a savory vegetable-potato chowder. A four-course tasting menu allows those who choose to dine Italian-style to savor the best of the kitchen.

Family parties chatter up a storm here, adding to the café's vivace, while couples, in twos and fours, place their names on the reservation list in anticipation of pleasing wine and a menu backed by friendly, informed service.

PUNCH NEAPOLITAN PIZZA

704 Cleveland Avenue South, Saint Paul
(651) 696-1066

Punch Express
3226 West Lake Street, Minneapolis (612) 929-0006
8353 Crystal Lake Road, Eden Prairie (952) 943-9557
$; F; O; no reservations

SAINT PAUL NATIVE John Soranno was growing a successful practice as a lawyer, but he'd spent his youth in Italy, where his father's business moved the family, and soon became afflicted with a love of true Italian pizza, which is something no law degree can cure. So in 1996 he traded his briefcase for a suitcase and set off for Naples to learn just how those pros had perfected the craft over the ages. Then he opened just such an authentic pizzeria back home in Highland Park.

Punch Express is named after Puncinella, a clown who symbolizes authenticity for the Associazione Vera Pizza Napoletana, or society of true pizza-makers of Naples, from which John took his inspiration. Like these masters, he uses only San Marzano tomatoes, Fior de Latte mozzarella, and a top-secret formula for that superior crust. But the true test of a master, he swears, is his skill with the wood-fired oven that produces those benchmark charred bubbles on the chewy crust.

Growing up in Milan, John joined the kids on the street for games of soccer, which, second only to pizza, soon became the love of his life. His servers are garbed in soccer shirts as they speed along the playing field of closely packed tables between the door—framed with awards too numerous to count—and the wood-fired oven, a red-hot icon in the rear.

Outside, a small deck, shaded by yellow umbrella tables, is separated by flower boxes from the driveway of the strip mall. Benches aside the entrance are packed with hopefuls waiting for tables (no reservations are taken, but one may phone ahead to be added to the seating list). Inside, under cheeky murals of Vesuvius erupting, Punch winking from behind his mask, and soccer symbols, tables are packed with a down-to-business crowd of young families, couples heading to the nearby movie, gaggles of girlfriends, and fellas toasting boys' night out—in other words, a true rainbow of pizza lovers, working their way through a topping list of 20 options. These are single-sized endeavors, not meant for sharing, John declares. John encourages his guests to devour them Italian-style, with knife and fork, because they're so richly laden.

Those who cannot bear the wait for the main event can start with an order of antipasti misti, a sampling of roasted vegetables, olives, and assorted meats and cheeses served with focaccia, adding a salad of their choosing—Caesar (of course), a lovely toss of Gorgonzola and walnuts upon romaine, or a lighter, mixed-green rendition. For those who must, there are a few desserts, almost as afterthoughts: bread pudding livened with sliced pears, a tiramisu mousse, and ice cream. And espresso, of course. The wine list is drawn from the winemakers of Naples to complement the pies. Moretti and Peroni head the short list of beers.

RISTORANTE LUCI

470 Cleveland Avenue South, Saint Paul
(651) 699-8258 • ristoranteluci.com
$$; reservations strongly recommended

IT'S ALL IN the *famiglia* here—a cramped family-run brick storefront in Highland Park starring some of the most authentic and artfully crafted Northern Italian cuisine in the entire region. After Al Smith's job as an executive for a manufacturing firm took him, his wife, and their brood of kids to Milan to live for a stretch, returning to a restaurant scene dominated by spaghetti and meatballs no longer filled the bill. So, almost in self-defense, Al and Lucille enlisted their kids and staked their future on their passion. They opened a tiny *ristorante* that introduced many a Minnesotan to top-quality comestibles, from Parmigiano Reggiano cheese to superior Barolo wines, among the elite foods of the country's north that found their way to the kitchen. Today, daughter Anna serves as wine maven and takes the lead in greeting guests.

The setting couldn't be more authentic, either, though it might not fill the travel-postcard image that we *Americani* may have in mind. The unassuming edifice, a former tavern, has been modestly transformed with swags of fabric furled in the tiny window and walls the color of caffé latte. Every last inch of valuable floor space is occupied by two rows of tables so closely packed that you often end up (again in true Italian fashion) talking with your neighbors and sharing morsels off their plates.

Honoring local producers—another Italian priority—the menu begins with a choice of antipasti, maybe homemade mozzarella with roasted bell pepper and tomato salad or polenta served with consommé and a pâté of Minnesota organic chicken. The soup of the day follows, along with a choice of mixed or Caesar salads. Then it's on to the primi, served in Italian, rather than Minnesotan, portion sizes: house-made fettucine with crab meat and citrus butter, the kitchen's fresh ravioli filled with spinach and ricotta, or a superior

SOLO VINO

517 Selby Avenue • Saint Paul • (651) 602-9515

The name says it all: Wine, and wine alone, is what this little shop is all about. It's the brainchild of a former bartender at Zander's Café next door, an opinionated expert on what a user-friendly wine shop should carry. He's since moved on, but under the current trio of vinophile owners, this still translates to lots and lots of interesting labels at less than $15 as well as the primo brands that bring tears to an aficionado's eyes. The spacious interior, lined with workmanlike shelves and racks constructed of raw timber, invites browsing, relaxing over a sample or two, and delving deeper into the whys and hows of a good fit with the dinner a patron has envisioned.

risotto boasting portobello mushrooms and mascarpone cheese among the grains of arborio rice.

Five secondi are next—scallops swimming in a truffled zabaglione with other exotic mushrooms; beef steak with truffle pesto; local Berkshire pork attended by whipped yams; Wild Acres chicken with yet more truffles scenting the clouds of whipped potatoes; and the fish of the evening. Sweets follow, along with a well-made cup of espresso. A *prezzo fisso* menu of four courses offers diners the option of somewhat smaller courses in order to sample more of the kitchen's skills. Wines, in a spectrum of price ranges, favor Italians, of course, abetted by a few select labels from California.

Families dine here in the early part of the evening, followed by couples seeking a romantic interlude or simply in search of an authentic experience. Whatever the case, reservations are essential.

SAJI YA

695 Grand Avenue, Saint Paul
(651) 292-0444 • www.sajiya.com
$$; O; P

SAJI YA IS THE life-support system of Grand Avenue's young and upwardbound who cannot make it through a day without their sushi. The restaurant's two sleight-of-hand slicers behind the special bar turn out several dozen varieties of nigiri (rice-based) morsels on demand, ranging from shrimp, tuna, and snapper to smoked eel, sea urchin, egg custard, and octopus. Their talents extend to fashioning maki sushi rolls as well, in another couple of dozen combinations. Sashimi rules here too, of course: choose tuna, yellow tail, or salmon.

Cranberry-red walls hung with Japanese brushstrokes form the backdrop to the serene setting, lit by moon-shaped paper lanterns winking above a miniature indoor pond complete with a gently arching bridge. A papier-mâché blowfish dangling from the dark ceiling slats offers little threat.

Venture across the miniature bridge to the back room's recesses, beside an on-view kitchen. In summertime, however, the second floor's outdoor balcony is where romantic couples head to catch the breeze.

Tempura—choose between shrimp or vegetarian versions—is the house specialty, served with salad, egg drop soup, and rice. Bento dinners widen the scope of options to include teriyaki chicken, salmon steak, and a husky rib eye, all served with crispy, stir-fried veggies.

But many patrons in the know simply graze among the appetizer listing to mix and match their meals. Ginger chicken wings marry nicely with a cold beer from Japan or a splash of saki. Soft-shell crab, squid, and grilled hamachi cheek are the seafood snacks, followed by beef tataki (tartare), plump gyozo dumplings, deep-fried tofu, and spicy Japanese pickles.

SIDNEY'S

Milton Mall, 917 Grand Avenue, Saint Paul
(651) 227-5000 • sidneysrestaurant.com
$–$$; F; P

Also Edina Galleria, Eagan, and Minnetonka locations

THE ORIGINAL SIDNEY'S—now a four-store Twin Cities success story—debuted over a decade ago, and the concept, as it has spread, remains just as attractive today. Here's the magic: Offer light and trendy, affordable and healthy food in a relaxed and comfortable format and add a Mediterranean aura to match the thrust of the winning menu.

Saint Paul's Grand Avenue store is the longest-running venue. It sets the stage for a relaxed meal with its Tuscan flavor, created with a terra cotta fountain in the public space, a baronial fireplace that could feed a village, heavy wooden ceiling beams, and terra cotta–style tiles paving an indoor courtyard that recreates the air of an Italian piazza. The warmth it conveys wins repeat visits from families with small children (whom Sidney accommodates with grace), couples enjoying casual date nights, and neighbors rendezvousing for a bite and chat.

The food fits today's modern outlook with its focus on fresh and healthful preparations, including many low-fat options, and a modern, in-and-out concept that doesn't strain the pocketbook. Sidney's hangs its chef's hat on its catalog of pizza and pasta offerings, each generous enough to guarantee a doggie bag.

The pizzas, fashioned from hand-tossed (watch them!) sourdough baked in a brick oven, take inspiration from all around the world. There's a classic Italian margherita with Roma tomatoes and mozzarella, an asparagus-brie number from who-knows-where (maybe the chef's keen imagination), and a pie showcasing grilled chicken in homemade barbecue sauce. Calzones and strombolis also have their day. Pastas again span the continents, from a spinach-mushroom ravioli and a classic fettucine Alfredo to a hot sausage and sweet pepper rendition straight from New Orleans, a Thai-inspired toss of linguine, and one of coconut chicken pumped with hot red curry on request.

Meal-sized salads, accompanied by a bread basket, range from a simple Caesar (conceived sans eggs to be kind to cholesterol-watchers) to a Danish blue cheese salad topped with shrimp; a Sausalito toss of chicken, poblanos, and salsa, served with guacamole dressing and crispy tortilla strips; or a Greek feast enhanced with feta cheese and kalamata olives. Or make a snack of starters. The artichoke dip is justly famous, and the mussels, crab cakes, and quesadillas have found their following, too.

Sidney's hearty entrées range from Santa Fe–roasted chicken with the café's signature skin-on mashed potatoes and grilled veggies to an ambitious veal Marsala, halibut in lemon-ginger sauce, or barbecued tenderloin of pork.

Some folks even manage dessert. They're not disappointed. Sidney's house specialty is its trademarked apple pie pizza, constructed upon a buttery crust, paddled into that brick oven, then served warm (of course!) with homemade caramel sauce and a scoop of vanilla Haagen-Dazs. If you must look elsewhere, consider the Georgia peach bread pudding overflowing with a bourbon-caramel sauce or the chocolate volcano cake decked with raspberry coulis. These definitely are designed for sharing.

Service is unremittingly friendly and fairly swift, which makes the sites a comfy venue for business lunches as well. And as a bonus, Sidney's serves breakfast seven days a week, another popular excuse to hold a business meeting.

TASTE OF THAILAND

1671 Selby Avenue, Saint Paul
(651) 644-3997 • tasteofthailandrestaurant.com
$–$$; F

IT'S SO SMALL you might drive right by, but that would be a big mistake. So, watch for the bright red awning and the neon "open" sign in the window of the unprepossessing little storefront on a quiet residential stretch of Merriam Park.

It's been run by the same kindly Thai family for 18 years, now a little more worn around the edges but not behind the stove. Fancy it's not. A few splashes of purple, the royal Thai color, on the low ceiling beams and wainscoting, along with a couple of traditional Thai musical instruments scattered here and there, is as far as ambience will take you. Booths line one room and tables fill the other, conveying the kind of character you remember from your parent's rec room.

But, chances are, your parents couldn't cook like this. Those booths and rows of tables are consistently crammed with flocks of repeat customers who

GRAND OLE CREAMERY

750 Grand Avenue • Saint Paul • (651) 293-1655
grandolecreamery.com

Grand Ole Creamy in 2004 celebrated its 20th anniversary of churning out award-winning ice creams (check out the many testimonial certificates framed on the walls). The tiny Grand Avenue shop is easy to spot by the lines snaking down the sidewalk on a hot summer day and folks making themselves at home on the old-fashioned street-side benches while they lustily slurp their cones. But time marches on, too. New items in 2004 included the New York ice cream sandwich, joining a litany of changing flavors—lemon torte to root beer sherbet, butter brickle to lime ice—to be scooped into your choice of waffle, sugar, or cake-style cone. (The aroma of sugar caramelizing as the cones bake permeates the Creamery, creating even more of an exercise in patience.) As a special prize, a malted milk ball awaits in the bottom of each cone.

show up for some of the undeniably best Thai food in town, backed by swift and friendly service.

The list is long, coded by symbols that denote "hot and spicy" (though that's negotiable, for everything is made to order), "house special," and "vegetarian." Appetizers lead off with egg rolls, spring rolls, and satays sided with an addictively spicy peanut curry sauce and cucumber salad, along with the even more enticing stuffed chicken wings or squid, plump with ground pork, silver thread noodles, shiitakes, and water chestnuts. Or go for the rice flour dumplings, pork steamed buns, or fish cakes livened with red curry paste and kaffir lime.

Wonton and egg drop soup, borrowed from Thailand's Asian neighbors, lead the list, but read on to discover stuffed cucumber soup and Tom Yum, the favorite: it melds lemongrass, straw mushrooms, the ginger-like galangal, kaffir lime leaves, and Thai chili peppers with your choice of protein.

Curries lead the list of entrées, and rightly so. The fish version combines coconut milk, red curry paste, kaffir lime leaves, and basil, while the masman curry melds its spices with beef, roasted peanuts, and potatoes. Many diners also are partial to the stir-fried shrimp in coconut-chili sauce or the crab legs stir-fried with hot chili peppers, fresh ginger, yellow curry, and crisp vegetables. Whole walleye, deep-fried, slathered with chili sauce, and sent out on a bed of lettuce, is another table-pleaser. Or choose your seafood steamed and served with spicy Thai salsa.

Papaya salad is almost a must here, thanks to its yin-yang meld of tart green fruit, chili peppers, fish sauce, dried shrimp, and peanuts, served with spicy dried beef and sticky rice. Fried rice and noodle dishes rate their own sublisting. And that's where you'll find the popular pad Thai, a soup-stew that's a meal in itself and almost the national dish. Sharing platters is the way to go, allowing a whole cast of flavors to pass your way.

And that includes desserts. Thai custard is the specialty, served solo or with buttercup squash (yes, it works) or sweet sticky rice. Or choose the sticky rice with mango and you won't go wrong, either.

W. A. FROST AND COMPANY

374 Selby Avenue, Saint Paul
(651) 224-5715 • wafrost.com
$$–$$$; O; P

HEARTS FLUTTER AT the very name. W. A. Frost, a longtime belle of historic Cathedral Hill, wins every poll as "most romantic" dining spot in town. The vintage red brick building that harks back to Victorian times—and which once, in fact, was a drug store—has charmed decades of return visitors who seek it out for business entertaining as well as the entertaining business of romance. Because it keeps late hours, it's also a destination for the ravenous after-theater crowd. Done up in volumes of lace and fringes, it boasts Persian carpets on its gleaming hardwood floors, Old Masters–style paintings winking from ornate gilded frames, and vintage cream brick walls that escalate to high ceilings overseeing marble-topped tables across which to hold—or shake—hands.

In wintertime, couples seek the cozy fireside tables, while in summer; Frost offers the best patio-dining ambience in the metro in a courtyard paved in bricks, under trees that seem to have flourished since the beginning of time amid a flock of flowerbeds.

The bad news: a while back, the food—overpriced and underwhelming—didn't live up to the setting. The good news: Current chef Russell Klein, a recent New York transplant, has remedied that situation. Oh, has he ever! And the wine list no longer requires a bank loan to enjoy. These days it sports interesting labels from South Africa to South America and beyond.

Under this kitchen's guidance, gravlax takes on new character when served with grapefruit, pink peppercorns, and tarragon. Other substantial starters

157

include wild Maine blue mussels swimming with chorizo in a spicy Moroccan broth or smoked Muscovy duck breast dressed with arugula-walnut pesto, pumpkin seed oil, and Parmesan cheese.

Entrées are just as hearty. Salmon arrives with savoy cabbage, applewood-smoked bacon, and golden potatoes at its side, competing against pan-roasted Wisconsin rabbit with roasted butternut squash, a potato-duck gratin, and a balsamic-fig reduction. Nor can you go far astray with the Pipestone, Minnesota-raised roast prime rib of pork, joined by parsnip mashed potatoes and grilled pears in an old-fashioned mustard sauce.

Desserts are just as haute-gone-homey: citrus-scented tapioca pudding, pear and cranberry cobbler, and homemade ice cream. Nostalgia fans also have the option of an over-the-top dessert from the "menu archives, circa 1985," such as espresso ice cream pie or a slice of the chocolate silk number.

This is one of the few kitchens around town that offers a cheese course—in fact, a choice of five superior selections, each with a wine suggestion. Or go for the sampling platter, served with preserved fruits. Frost also offers a choice of four genres of coffee beans.

The adjoining barroom, convivial as always, proffers its own, more informal menu of meal-sized salads, burgers, sandwiches, and such, also available on the patio. Service, under the new regime, makes diners feel like treasured guests.

ZANDER CAFE

525 Selby Avenue, Saint Paul
(651) 222-5224
$$; M

WHEN ZANDER OPENED a few years back, the sound heard throughout the metro was a collective sigh of relief. Chef-owner Alexander Dixon—"Zander" to one and all—had brightened many a notable kitchen (New French Café, Rosewood Room, Faegre's, to mention a few for those whose zest for imaginative cooking goes back a decade), then fell off the radar when he left town.

Well, he's back where he belongs again, and for the first time, he's his own boss. After all those dress rehearsals in the limelight, he knew what he wanted (and what we wanted, too) and got it right.

The small, cozy cream-brick structure carries his name on a marquee of turquoise blue—a good sign of the upbeat but laid-back nature of the pair of rooms it heralds. Pushing through the heavy copper metal door, patrons immediately spot a tiny stage at the rear, complete with a compact piano, where live music adds to the ambient flavor on weekend evenings. Diners can savor the chanteuse du jour while sampling what the kitchen has in store, snuggling back into the curvy, multicolored booths or perched at a half-moon cocktail table.

Cross through to the quieter room, which is geared for more serious dining (as is the alcove grafted to its farther side), with bare tabletops and spare décor under a collation of industrial pipes in the shadows of the ceiling. The company of diners consists of hip denizens of this regentrified neighborhood, as forward as the setting (but not in a test-your-cool capacity: after all, this is Saint Paul, where the mantra of "got it but don't flaunt it" reigns). It's a generational stew of slackers, thirtysomethings, boomers, and beyond, united in animated conversation as well as allegiance to Zander's culinary concept.

Many diners begin by dipping their spoons into the chef's signature Three Soup Mosaic, arranged in the same bowl, served hot or chilled, depending on the season. Then it's on to appetizers, where the menu shimmers with the likes of duck confit in puff pastry, a Maryland blue crab cake served with Louis sauce, and a collage of Saint Pete's local blue cheese paired with roasted beets. Salads follow, as does the artisan cheese of the day (or save it to finish off the evening).

Flip the menu to discover two avenues to pursue. The Casual Dining listing leads folks to fare like salmon steamed in parchment, served with a lemon hollandaise; penne pasta in a peppery spinach cream sauce flagged with figs and raisins under a topping of pine nuts, black olives, and goat cheese; or perhaps a Caribbean chicken stew freshened with kale and collard greens. Or steer your selection to the entrées, with dishes such as curried chicken; what Zander calls the jambalaya, fueled with his homemade XXX hot sauce; or a pepper-crusted pork chop in a Riesling and dried cherry sauce alongside Gruyere croquettes.

And then there's the wine list, which is also out of the ordinary. (Remember, the café stands next door to Solo Vino, see page 152.) Servers are of the non-stuffy breed who simply aim to be your temporary friend and mentor. And in this sweet café, it works.

CHAPTER SEVEN

Worth the Drive

BAYPORT COOKERY

328 5th Avenue North, Bayport
(651) 430-1066 • bayportcookery.com
$$–$$$; reservations required

BAYPORT IS A MODEST little riverside community Twin Cities folks might pass right through en route to Stillwater—unless they're foodies. Those in the know pull a left off Main Street to head to the Bayport Cookery. It's a tiny storefront, unassuming from the outside but assuming a whole lot within its minuscule kitchen. For years the dining space has been small as well, just a handful of tables for its dinner-only service; and just beyond an interior window wall there is also a room for private parties or functions by corporations such as Bayport-based Andersen Windows, whose execs delight in revealing a hideaway of haute cuisine to visitors who assume they're stuck with forgettable dining in flyover land.

But recently chef-owner Jim Kyndberg added an à la carte list to his prix fixe format and doubled the badly needed floor space to include a second, larger room centered on a blazing fireplace. He also hired a cooking team lured from the esteemed Rivertown Inn in Stillwater. Patrick O'Toole, as chef de cuisine under Kyndberg, oversees the à la carte menu, and his wife, Ronna, serves as pastry chef. Together the team pays homage to local growers and procurers whenever they can—indeed, they're known to forage wild ferns and herbs and berries to create complex courses inspired by O'Toole's stints in California, their combined travels, and, mainly, their unique spirit of invention.

The new menu salutes starters such as a salad of field greens spangled with beets, apples, pears, toasted hazelnuts, and a dollop of warm goat cheese; soups that segue from a complex seafood gumbo to a comfortable bowl of squash puree; and a luxurious starter of foie gras topped with a sea scallop, all set upon chestnut puree drizzled with truffle oil. (Dishes don't come more over the top than that in this region.)

Entrées include duck with wild mushrooms atop house-made fettucine; a reappearance of the sea scallops, this time paired with basmati rice and sauced with passion fruit; and a pork tenderloin sliced over risotto mined with smoky bacon.

Yes, those five- and nine-course prix fixe meals are still available as well. A typical feast may begin with cioppino broth that warms swordfish, mussels, and tempura shrimp. The soup prepares the palate for brined pork loin seared in smoked applewood bacon, served over pickled radicchio, followed by Muscovy duck soup lush with root vegetables, spinach, and shiitake mushrooms.

The main event might be lamb aside a gratin of celery root, green apple, and quinoa pilaf, all plated with a balsamic pomegranate reduction. And for dessert, a finale such as a mixed berry tart with chestnut streusel and tangerine ice cream is proposed to satisfy one's sweet tooth.

Service is folksy, not formal, and can provide a bit of a pause, but one doesn't drive out here to be rushed, anyway. Instead, sip a choice wine from Bayport Cookery's list of select labels and relax.

The Cookery is known for its festival weeks—seasonal menus that hail a special ingredient, such as morel mushrooms or garlic (yes, even featured in the dessert, and it works). Game is likely to appear in autumn. And adventure every month of the year.

CESARE'S WINE BAR

102 South 2nd Street, Stillwater
(651) 439-1352 • cesareswinebar.com
$–$$; P; O

CESARE'S WINE BAR was born of necessity, they swear. When its four founders, foodies to the core, asked fellow aficionados of fine wines where they went out to eat, they heard this: "We don't. In restaurants, a $50 bottle of wine costs $120."

That's all the market research it took. Clearly there was a following waiting to happen, so Richard Lay and Kiersten Lysne allied with Leslie and Robert Alexander to launch the most radical wine bar in the region. As crusaders, first they put together a wine list divided by grape varietals (thus, under Sangiovese you'll find both paisano Chianti and lordly Brunello), sans the usual wine-speak verbiage. What you won't find are the big name brands; rather, they offer over 350 labels of little-known, boutique producers from around the world favored by the owners. (In fact, Robert Alexander named the place after a tiny producer with whom he'd worked in Italy.) Also almost unheard of: Any bottle on the list can be tried by the glass if two glasses are ordered. And most revolutionary of all, the markup over wholesale wine prices is a skinny 1.8 percent.

Patrons may make tasting notes on their personal copies of the list, which they can stash with the staff till their next visit. "We let our guests do the talking," Alexander notes, "we don't tell people what to like. Here, there's no such thing as a 'stupid' question. We greet them with open arms."

Alexander is the home builder-turned-sommelier who converted Stillwater's former newspaper office into the cheery bar cum café. It's an ode to fine woods from around the globe, including wine boxes incorporated into tabletops. A wine cellar to one side serves as a site of private dinners; classes regularly are offered, too.

Leslie Alexander, whose background includes cooking stints with the D'Amico corporation, has fashioned a small and select menu to accompany the wines. Her cheese plate is a special hit, and she's a stickler for incorporating special finds from small producers. Flights of olive oil, served with fresh bread, are another edible educational opportunity.

Leslie describes her menu as "Mediterranean with a nod toward Italy"—and a nod toward the small, local artisan procurers to whom she pays loyalty. Two pizzas lead the dinner list, followed by a choice of salads and soup of the day and a duet of pastas that often stars linguine with walnut-sage pesto. More substantial entrées, which change weekly, curry diners' favor with fare like apple- and basil-poached halibut upon potato pancakes and apple-jicama slaw; a rack of lamb with sweet onion marmalade; risotto topped with house-roasted tomatoes; or a rustic panzanella (bread) salad drizzled with aged balsamic vinegar and the finest olive oil. Baker that the lady is, desserts here are not to be scorned. A strawberry napoleon constructed with vanilla-bean cream and almond shortbread won't disappoint.

In summertime, umbrella tables on the deck allow for ogling the historic buildings of this pretty river town.

MARX WINE BAR AND GRILL

241 South Main Street, Stillwater
(651) 439-8333 • marx.com
$–$$

WELCOME TO MARX, decidedly the most trendy design statement in all of Stillwater, a small town more renowned for its vintage rather than its forward trappings. Although the tiny bistro occupies one of those signature Main Street storefronts from the 1800s, its statement is directed clearly toward the future. The Jetsons would be right at home here, gathered at one of the eye-catching Formica-topped tables in glowing red that vibrate against walls of chartreuse and cobalt. The artworks that punctuate that colorful vision are showcased in black frames hung jauntily off-kilter and lit by dangling globes of brilliant blue. A glossy green drape divides the cluster of tables from the tiny bar.

The arresting décor, done on a modest budget, was marshaled by chef-owner Mark Hanson, who ran the nearby vintage Harvest Inn before debuting Marx in 2002. It's been a magnet for food and wine cognoscenti ever since, as well as simply a comfy hangout for couples drawn in by its inviting presence.

The wine list offers close to three dozen eclectic labels, all available by the glass as well as by the bottle. It makes for good grazing, as does the wide-ranging and appealing menu. Start with nibbles like fresh, homemade mozzarella paired with basil and tomatoes; creamy, bite-sized dumplings of walleye and hot chili, seasoned with sweet potato and Spanish spices; or bruschetta with a choice of worldwide toppings. Add a salad, perhaps curly endive dotted with bacon and Gorgonzola under a shower of candied pecans and roasted beets or warm goat cheese with roasted tomatoes.

Many folks head straight for the list of plate-sized pizzas. Pasta fanciers pursue a list that leads off with Italian classics, then breaks rank with dishes like a toss of Parmigiana, pistachios, and cream or linguine tangled with shrimp, basil, tomatoes, and a spritz of vodka in the sauce.

The grills are where Mark of Marx really shines. Contemplate a memorable osso buco on creamy, mushroom-studded polenta surrounded with colorful vegetables of the season, for starters. Or porcini-crusted chicken with fava-bean pesto and grilled asparagus. Filet fanciers consider the cut of beef with caramelized onions, fennel, and a red wine reduction to be about as good as it gets. And there's always a daily fish special.

And always desserts. Chocolate leads the list, fashioned into a truffle cake served with warm truffle sauce and freshly beaten cream. And the warm banana cake served with bananas, caramel, and cream is considered a mighty close second. Portions are generous enough to pass around the table, if you can bear to let the plate out of your grasp.

THE PORT

Saint James Hotel, 406 Main Street, Red Wing
(651) 388-2846 • st-james-hotel.com
$$–$$$; P

SOME PEOPLE HEAD to Red Wing to bike the Cannon River Trail; others to scour the outlet malls and antiques shops; and just about everybody to capture leaf-watching at its prime. These days the colors on autumn's turning maples almost take a back seat to those on the plate of The Port, the dining room of the vintage Saint James Hotel.

The romantic, red-brick hotel, overlooking a bend in the Mississippi where pleasure boats lie anchored, has long been a favorite getaway for honey-

ALEXIS BAILLY WINERY

18200 Kirby Avenue • Hastings, Minnesota • (651) 437-1413

The name is French, and so are many of the grape varietals, such as the signature Marechal Foch and Seyval, but the winemaker is 100 percent Minnesotan. Nan Bailly, vintner and proprietor of Alexis Bailly Winery, with her flame-red hair and resounding laugh, is a striking presence amid the rolling green acres of vineyards, which are located just outside of Hastings. Nan's father, a Twin Cities attorney, planted the vines and built the winery to pursue a dream. She got on-the-job training by working alongside her father daily in the early days of the winery, and upon his death Nan was all the more determined to show the world what his favorite grapes could do.

Is Bacchus laughing, or what? This is the only winery that must bury its vines six feet under the snow each winter and then flaunt the project on its label: "Where the grapes must suffer." Apparently the masochism pays off, for the vintages are winning medals in competitions and appearing on restaurant wine lists; they also fly out the cellar door when customers come to shop. A sweet, orange-infused dessert wine, Ratafia, is particularly popular.

The winery is open from 11 a.m. to 5:30 p.m. Friday through Sunday, May through November. Alas, no tours.

mooners and couples celebrating anniversaries, but the question loomed: Where to eat?

After some years lying becalmed in the culinary waters, The Port is once again producing exemplary regional cooking. It's reinstated itself as the a destination for Red Wing's townies, holding hands across the table, and someplace worthy where astute owners of Red Wing's many bed and breakfasts can direct their guests.

The below-stairs room is as warm and welcoming as the hold of a ship with a dark-beamed ceiling, photos of old riverboats, a Swedish fireplace, soft lighting, crisp linen, and slowly melting candles.

The appetizer list is the first indication that this is no ordinary hotel kitchen. Shrimp cocktail, sure—everybody does that. But here it's spiked with daikon and cilantro. Smoked salmon? Yeah, right. Well, look again: the silky slices come partnered with grilled asparagus and a confit of plum tomatoes.

Then there's the croustade of wild mushrooms, doubly enhanced with a vanilla-balsamic sauce and a truffle-oil hollandaise. Or, with a hint from the southern end of the Mississippi, there are Cajun turnovers cosseting chicken and andouille sausage in a piquant Louisiana sauce. And the butternut squash ravioli, strewn with toasted pumpkin seeds, are worth the drive alone. Soups range from a suave French onion glazed with cheese to a perky pepper pot adrift with spaetzle.

Who can resist the state's official fish, the walleye, when presented as it is here, crusted with almonds and sided with an apple-fennel risotto and ginger-apricot sauce? Only the hardy. But then they've probably got their eyes fastened on the rack of lamb upon herbed couscous under a Bing cherry bordelaise. Or the double prime rib of pork, abetted by smoked bacon and green cabbage in a diablo sauce. Or the magic the kitchen performs on a simple chicken breast, dressed for success in a fig-Madeira sauce and served with leek and mushroom bread pudding. Still others make it a point to mark their calendars for Tuesday, the day the roast duck is offered with apple, craisin, and wild rice stuffing and a brandied apple glaze. And surf-and-turfers know that Thursday is the steak and lobster night.

Fortunately or unfortunately, depending on your personal trainer's advice, desserts are just as delicious. Consider blueberry crème brûlée, and self-control flies out the window. In season, the old-fashioned baking powder biscuit shortcake overflows with strawberries, blueberries, and more, lazing on a mango-blueberry coulis under an avalanche of whipped cream. It's a good port to come to for shelter these days.

SAN PEDRO CAFÉ

426 Second Street, Hudson, Wisconsin
(715) 389-4003
$$; O; F; no reservations

IT MAY BE SNOWING outside, as it seems to much of the year in Hudson, but the tropical sizzle pulsing from San Pedro provides the perfect antidote to cabin fever. No reservations are taken, so you'll spot the popular hangout by lines forming at the door.

It's a historic door at that. Owner Pete Foster of Barker's Landing, Inc. (which operated another lively local favorite, Barker's Bar and Grill, across the street), has preserved many of the original fixtures of this vintage brick building on the town's main street, erected in 1879 as this riverside city's premier bank.

Pete, in love with the tropics, named and themed his café after a small town he'd discovered near Belize. The menu pays homage to a multitude of its Caribbean neighbors, too, with the added focus of an open, wood-fired brick oven that imparts a sweet-smoky flavor to almost anything in sight, from the café's ample breakfast muffins to the pizzas paddled in as diners at the counter salivate, to game and fish and even veggies before they're run to waiting booths and tables.

San Pedro's appetizers set the mood. Guests may dig into lobster and scallop seviche with fresh lime, habanero peppers, and cilantro; Jamaican jerk chicken tenders, served with watermelon salsa and banana-guava dipping sauce; or smoked duckling nachos lit with the kitchen's homemade pico de gallo and topped with a hopping habanero aioli and tropical mango salsa.

Those wood-fired pizzas take their names from sunny island destinations. The Trinidad number blends wild mushrooms with sauteed spinach, mozzarella, and a smoked chili-cilantro sauce, while the Curaçao calls on kalamata olives, roasted sweet red peppers, wild mushrooms, artichoke hearts, and goat cheese atop the kitchen's tomato sauce.

Pastas prove just as lively. Rasta Pasta mingles jerk-spiced, wood-roasted chicken with garlic and serrano peppers in a sweet pepper broth before they're tossed with penne and tomatoes. Chicken fettucine with chili cream sauce calls on wood-roasted vegetables as well. Each is accompanied by a green salad in mango vinaigrette and fresh-baked ciabatta bread.

But it's the wood-roasted meat and seafood specialties that make the chef's heart beat faster. Chef Christopher Ray, a vocal advocate of Prairie cuisine, particularly loves to stock his larder with game. He's prepared it as guest chef everywhere from the U.S. Naval Academy to America's Pork Producers. Voted a Rising Young Chef of Wisconsin by the state's Restaurant Association, he's also produced a cookbook called *The Wild Menu*, featuring his beloved game.

Here he lends these skills to entrées such as barbecue and mustard-crusted beef tenderloin, garnished with smoked chili-cilantro sauce and charred red onions; Yucatan pork stew, simmered with vegetables, serrano peppers, and roasted garlic, served with red beans and rice; and tortilla-crusted grouper, drizzled with banana-guava sauce, garnished with that tasty watermelon salsa and sided with beans and rice. Shrimp Monique celebrates huge tiger shellfish in a Jamaican jerk marinade, finished with a rosemary-fig chutney and served with his now-famous banana mashed potatoes. The dress code is casual, as befits the tropics. And if you've mislaid your T-shirt, sweatshirt, jacket, chef's cap, or even coffee mug, not to worry: All such items are for sale as souvenirs of your visit.

SAVORIES BISTRO

108 North Main Street, Stillwater
(651) 430-0702 • savoriesbistro.com
$$; F

IT'S BEYOND REASON to encounter a classically-trained chef and a pastry diva in a small town café, but Stillwater isn't your average dot on the map, and Jeffrey and Kirstin Klemetsrud are not your ordinary kitchen duo. The husband and wife team have traveled abroad extensively; he's studied at the Holy of Holies (a.k.a, the Culinary Institute of America), and she helped put Saint Paul's Cafe Latte on everyone's A-list with her fine pastries.

Into their second decade as restaurateurs on their own, the pair has expanded and upgraded—ever so slightly—the Main Street storefront that lures locals and city folks alike. It wears the casual, homey look of a Provençal bistro with candles glimmering against burgundy walls in both small rooms and servers who are as sweet as they are accomplished.

What hasn't changed is the couple's dedication to seasonal bounty from local, often organic, producers on their monthly changing menu and their insistence that everything be made in-house, from stocks and soups to salad dressings and, of course, Kirsten's elite breads and pastries.

Breakfast, served weekends only, is a leisurely affair, whether it's simply a cappuccino with your newspaper or one of the four starring omelets, with fillings like confetti corn and asparagus with boursin cheese, or perhaps a flaky cornmeal johnnycake with raspberry butter and real maple syrup, stuffed soufflé French toast, or deep-dish quiche. The lunch list segues from hearty sandwiches and salads to interesting pastas and such.

It's at dinner that their chosen epithet of "global metropolitan" cooking really shines. This is earthy fare, not precious stuff, like homemade potted pork with coriander and fennel served with tomato chutney as a starter. Or begin with salmon spring rolls sided with coconut sambal and spicy peanut sauce, or Tunisian shrimp cocktail laced with harissa. A dish of stuffed portobellos in homemade puff pastry with French apple cider sauce is one indication of the intriguing fare vegetarians can expect.

Entrées prove even more adventurous, with the likes of tapenade-crusted rack of lamb with Moroccan honey and cumin-charred carrot gratin, or maybe a dilled game hen wrapped in a rasher of bacon, or a garlicky lamb pot pie with cheddar-mustard crust.

Let's not forget Kirsten's desserts, presented on a rustic copper tray to make deciding even more difficult. Take a gander at the buttermilk panna cotta with three-berry compote, the raspberry and Drambuie trifle, the chocolate-raspberry truffle cake, and the Milky Way and chocolate short-bread tart. Then let 'er rip! The wine list is every bit as interesting, and it's half-price on Tasting Tuesdays.

RESTAURANTS BY CUISINE

ASIAN
Chino Latino
Fuji Ya
Origami
Rainbow
Rice Paper
Ruam Mit
Saji Ya
Sakura
Sawatdee
Taste of Thailand
Yummy

BARBECUE
Dixies
Famous Dave's
Market

ECLECTIC
Auriga
Bakery on Grand
Bobino
Bryant Lake Bowl
Café Barbette
Café Brenda
Café Latte
Café 28
Chino Latino
Corner Table
French Meadow
Levain
Loring Pasta Bar
Marx
Modern
Nochee
Oddfellows
128 Café
POP!
Sapor
Savories
Sidney's
SkyRoom
Tryg's
Zander

FRENCH
A Rebours
La Fougasse
Louis XIII
Vincent

GERMAN, MIDDLE EUROPEAN, AND EASTERN EUROPEAN
Black Forest
Nye's

GREEK AND MIDDLE EASTERN
Christos
Fhima's
Gardens of Salonika
It's Greek to Me
Kafe 421
Khyber Pass

INDIAN
New Delhi
Udupi

IRISH
Local, The

ITALIAN
Al Vento
Bellanotte
Broders
Buca di Beppo
Campiello
Cesare's
D'Amico Cucina
Figlio
Giorgio's
La Grolla
Luci Ancora
Pane Vino Dolce
Pazzaluna
Prima
Ristorante Luci

MEXICAN/LATIN
Babalu
Bar Abilene
Chino Latino
La Bodega

173

Mojito
Morelos
San Pedro
Solera
Tejas

PIZZA
Green Mill
Pizza Luce
Punch
Sidney's

REGIONAL AMERICAN
510
Bar Abilene
Bayport Cookery
Café Lurcat
California Café
Convention Grill
Cosmos
Craftsman, The
Dakota
Dixies
Famous Dave's
Firelake
Goodfellow's
Heartland
Ikes's
Jax
jP American Bistro
Kinkaid's
Levain
Lexington, The
Lord Fletcher's

Lucia's
McCormick & Schmick's
Mission
Modern
Monte Carlo
Napa Valley Grille
Nye's
Palomino
Peter's Grill
Port, The
Restaurant Alma
Sample Room
St. Paul Grill
Tryg's
W. A. Frost

SEAFOOD
Jax
Kincaid's
McCormick & Schmick's
Oceanaire

STEAK
Casper's Cherokee Sirloin Room
Jax
Manny's
Morton's
Murray's

VEGETARIAN
Café Brenda
Udupi

Family Friendly Spots

Broders
Buca
Café 28
Convention Grill
Famous Dave's
French Meadow
Gardens of Salonika
It's Greek to Me
Jax
Market Bar-B-Que

Monte Carlo
Morelos
POP!
Prima
Rainbow
SkyRoom
Tejas
Udupi
Yummy

Intimate Dining

128 Café
A Rebours
Al Vento
Auriga
Bakery on Grand
Bayport American Cookery
Café Barbette
Café Brenda
Cafe 28
Cesare's
Corner Table
Craftsman, The
Heartland

jP American Bistro
Kafe 421
Levain
Marx
Modern
Oddfellows
POP!
Prima
Restaurant Alma
Sample Room
Sapor
Savories
Zander

Live Entertainment

Babalu
Bellanotte
Bryant Lake Bowl
Café Lurcat
Dakota
D'Amico Cucina
Famous Dave's

Fhima's
La Bodega
Loring Pasta Bar
Nochee
Nye's
Zander

Outdoor Seating

Al Vento
Auriga
Bar Abilene
Black Forest
Bobino
Café Barbette
Café 28
Campiello
Cesare's
Dakota
Dixies
Figlio
French Meadow
Giorgio
It's Greek to Me
Jax
jP American Bistro

La Bodega
La Fougasse
La Grolla
Local
Lord Fletcher's
Loring Pasta Bar
Lucia's
McCormick & Schmick's
Punch
Restaurant Alma
Saji Ya
San Pedro
Sapor
Solera
Tejas
Tryg's
W. A. Frost

Romantic Settings

A Rebours
Bayport Cookery
Cosmos
D'Amico Cucina
Fhima's
510
La Grolla
Loring Pasta Bar
Louis XIII
Pane Vino Dolce
Port
Solera

Great for Special Occasions

510
Bayport Cookery
Cosmos
D'Amico Cucina
Goodfellow's
Jax
Kincaid's
Manny's
Morton's
Murray's
Oceanaire
Pazzaluna
Port
St. Paul Grill
Vincent

Trendy/Singles' Favorites

Babalu
Bar Abilene
Bellanotte
Bobino
Bryant Lake Bowl
Café Lurcat
Chino Latino
Dakota
Fhima's
La Bodega
Local
Mojito
Solera
Tryg's

INDEX

More Great Titles

FROM TRAILS BOOKS & PRAIRIE OAK PRESS

ACTIVITY GUIDES

Biking Wisconsin: 50 Great Road and Trail Rides, *Steve Johnson*

Great Cross-Country Ski Trails: Wisconsin, Minnesota, Michigan & Ontario, *Wm. Chad McGrath*

Great Iowa Walks: 50 Strolls, Rambles, Hikes, and Treks, *Lynn L. Walters*

Great Midwest Country Escapes, *Nina Gadowski*

Great Minnesota Walks: 49 Strolls, Rambles, Hikes, and Treks, *Wm. Chad McGrath*

Great Wisconsin Walks: 45 Strolls, Rambles, Hikes, and Treks, *Wm. Chad McGrath*

Horsing Around in Wisconsin, *Anne M. Connor*

Iowa Underground, *Greg A. Brick*

Minnesota Underground & the Best of the Black Hills, *Doris Green*

Paddling Illinois: 64 Great Trips by Canoe and Kayak, *Mike Svob*

Paddling Iowa: 96 Great Trips by Canoe and Kayak, *Nate Hoogeveen*

Paddling Northern Minnesota: 86 Great Trips by Canoe and Kayak, *Lynne Smith Diebel*

Paddling Northern Wisconsin: 82 Great Trips by Canoe and Kayak, *Mike Svob*

Paddling Southern Wisconsin: 82 Great Trips by Canoe and Kayak, *Mike Svob*

Walking Tours of Wisconsin's Historic Towns, *Lucy Rhodes, Elizabeth McBride, Anita Matcha*

Wisconsin's Outdoor Treasures: A Guide to 150 Natural Destinations, *Tim Bewer*

Wisconsin Underground, *Doris Green*

TRAVEL GUIDES

Classic Wisconsin Weekends, *Michael Bie*

County Parks of Minnesota, *Timothy J. Engrav*

Great Indiana Weekend Adventures, *Sally McKinney*

Great Iowa Weekend Adventures, *Mike Whye*

Great Little Museums of the Midwest, *Christine des Garennes*

Great Minnesota Taverns, *David K. Wright & Monica G. Wright*

Great Minnesota Weekend Adventures, *Beth Gauper*

Great Weekend Adventures, *the Editors of Wisconsin Trails*

Great Wisconsin Romantic Weekends, *Christine des Garennes*

Great Wisconsin Taverns: 101 Distinctive Badger Bars, *Dennis Boyer*

Iowa's Hometown Flavors, *Donna Tabbert Long*

The Great Indiana Touring Book: 20 Spectacular Auto Trips, *Thomas Huhti*

Sacred Sites of Minnesota, *John-Brian Paprock & Teresa Peneguy Paprock*

Sacred Sites of Wisconsin, *John-Brian Paprock & Teresa Peneguy Paprock*

Tastes of Minnesota: A Food Lover's Tour, *Donna Tabbert Long*
The Great Iowa Touring Book: 27 Spectacular Auto Trips, *Mike Whye*
The Great Minnesota Touring Book: 30 Spectacular Auto Trips, *Thomas Huhti*
The Great Wisconsin Touring Book: 30 Spectacular Auto Tours, *Gary Knowles*
Wisconsin Family Weekends: 20 Fun Trips for You and the Kids,
Susan Lampert Smith
Wisconsin Golf Getaways, *Jeff Mayers and Jerry Poling*
Wisconsin Lighthouses: A Photographic and Historical Guide,
Ken and Barb Wardius
Wisconsin's Hometown Flavors, *Terese Allen*
Wisconsin Waterfalls, *Patrick Lisi*
Up North Wisconsin: A Region for All Seasons, *Sharyn Alden*

HOME & GARDEN
Bountiful Wisconsin: 110 Favorite Recipes, *Terese Allen*
Codfather 2, *Jeff Hagen*
Creating a Perennial Garden in the Midwest, *Joan Severa*
Eating Well in Wisconsin, *Jerry Minnich*
Foods That Made Wisconsin Famous: 150 Great Recipes, *Richard J. Baumann*
Midwest Cottage Gardening, *Frances Manos*
North Woods Cottage Cookbook, *Jerry Minnich*
Wisconsin Country Gourmet, *Marge Snyder & Suzanne Breckenridge*
Wisconsin Garden Guide, *Jerry Minnich*
Wisconsin Wildfoods: 100 Recipes for Badger State Bounties, *John Motouiloff*

HISTORICAL BOOKS
Duck Hunting on the Fox: Hunting and Decoy-Carving Traditions,
Stephen M. Miller
Grand Army of the Republic: Department of Wisconsin, *Thomas J. McCrory*
Portrait of the Past: A Photographic Journey Through Wisconsin 1865-1920,
Howard Mead, Jill Dean, and Susan Smith
Prairie Whistles: Tales of Midwest Railroading, *Dennis Boyer*
Shipwrecks of Lake Michigan, *Benjamin J. Shelak*
Wisconsin At War: 20th Century Conflicts Through the Eyes of Veterans,
Dr. James F. McIntosh, M.D.
Wisconsin's Historic Houses & Living History Museums, *Krista Finstad Hanson*

GIFT BOOKS
Celebrating Door County's Wild Places, *The Ridges Sanctuary*
Fairlawn: Restoring the Splendor, *Tom Davis*
Madison, *Photography by Brent Nicastro*
Milwaukee, *Photography by Todd Dacquisto*

Spirit of the North: A Photographic Journey Through Northern Wisconsin,
Richard Hamilton Smith
The Spirit of Door County: A Photographic Essay, *Darryl R. Beers*
Uncommon Sense: The Life Of Marshall Erdman, *Doug Moe & Alice D'Alessio*

LEGENDS & LORE
Driftless Spirits: Ghosts of Southwest Wisconsin, *Dennis Boyer*
Haunted Wisconsin, *Michael Norman and Beth Scott*
The Beast of Bray Road: Tailing Wisconsin's Werewolf, *Linda S. Godfrey*
The Eagle's Voice: Tales Told by Indian Effigy Mounds, *Gary J. Maier, M.D.*
The Poison Widow: A True Story of Sin, Strychnine, & Murder, *Linda S. Godfrey*
The W-Files: True Reports of Wisconsin's Unexplained Phenomena, *Jay Rath*

YOUNG READERS
ABCs Naturally, *Lynne Smith Diebel & Jann Faust Kalscheur*
ABCs of Wisconsin, *Dori Hillestad Butler, Illustrated by Alison Relyea*
H is for Hawkeye, *Jay Wagner, Illustrated by Eileen Potts Dawson*
H is for Hoosier, *Dori Hillestad Butler, Illustrated by Eileen Potts Dawson*
Wisconsin Portraits, *Martin Hintz*
Wisconsin Sports Heroes, *Martin Hintz*
W is for Wisconsin, *Dori Hillestad Butler, Illustrated by Eileen Potts Dawson*

SPORTS
Always a Badger: The Pat Richter Story, *Vince Sweeney*
Baseball in Beertown: America's Pastime in Milwaukee, *Todd Mishler*
Before They Were the Packers: Green Bay's Town Team Days,
Denis J. Gullickson & Carl Hanson
Cold Wars: 40+ Years of Packer-Viking Rivalry, *Todd Mishler*
Downfield: Untold Stories of the Green Bay Packers, *Jerry Poling*
Great Moments in Wisconsin Sports, *Todd Mishler*
Green Bay Packers Titletown Trivia Teasers, *Don Davenport*
Mean on Sunday: The Autobiography of Ray Nitschke, *Robert W. Wells*
Mudbaths and Bloodbaths: The Inside Story of the Bears-Packers Rivalry,
Gary D'Amato & Cliff Christl
Packers By the Numbers: Jersey Numbers and the Players Who Wore Them,
John Maxymuk

For a free catalog, phone, write, or e-mail us.

Trails Books
P.O. Box 317, Black Earth, WI 53515
(800) 236-8088 • e-mail: books@wistrails.com